Once We Were Eight

To Leon,
A slice of my history,
Zachor - Remember
Ray [illegible]

Edited by Mary Ann Cooper
Cover Design by Meredith Cooper
First Edition: 2014
Printed in the United States of America
ISBN: 978 1 6203 0852 3

Once We Were Eight

By

Raymond Fishler

Dedicated to my wife, Rhoda, my children, David and Laura, my son-in-law, Ronen and my grandchildren, Brian, Melissa, Ariel and Daniel.

Table of Contents

Acknowledgements

After almost 75 years since the start of World War II, and after many attempts to record my wartime memories, I have finally mustered my emotional strength, gathered my thoughts and put them on paper. This task was not easy, but is important to me for many reasons. I feel that my story needs to be told for future generations so that they can learn from the Holocaust. This book is also my legacy to those that survived and the millions of men, women and children who did not. During the war years, we did not have the "luxury" of grieving for our lost loved ones. This book is my way of expressing my love for my lost family members, and my grief for all those lives that were cut short because of hate, prejudice and intolerance.

I am indebted to many who encouraged and supported me during this process. My daughter, Laura, despite her very busy schedule found time to conduct research, write, edit and encourage me along the way. Her husband, Ronen, and sons, Ariel and Daniel, also supported me every inch of the way. My son, David, and his children, Brian and Melissa, through the years have listened patiently to my stories encouraging me to record them so that they would have them on record for themselves and for future generations.

I want to thank my friend, Edna Casapulla, for her professional expertise and for introducing my wife to Mary Ann Cooper. Mary Ann assisted me in writing this memoir. Her endless patience, persistence, diligence, professionalism and skill are greatly appreciated. Her daughter, Meredith Cooper, was responsible for the book's cover design, artwork and photos. I am also thankful to her for her understanding, patience and skill.

I want to thank my wife, Rhoda, who was the driving force behind this effort. She read and re-read every line, spending hours writing, editing, and encouraging me to undertake this satisfying but painful task, to ensure that this book – my dream – would come to fruition. Without her support and persistence, I would not and could not have written this memoir.

My bedroom window (right) overlooking my garden

Prologue

I believe that I'm a lucky man. Some people are confused when I say this because of everything I've experienced in my life. They wonder how I can consider myself to be so fortunate after facing the senseless loss of my family and friends to hate and bigotry during WWII. But I'm here and that says it all. There have been many moments in my life when I could have died and should have died, but I was spared. Who knows why? Perhaps I'm here to speak for others who weren't so lucky. Many people were leading happy and productive lives in my town, my country, and throughout Europe, until they experienced the horrific things that people are capable of doing to their fellow human beings. That's why it's important for me to tell my story.

On the last day of August 1939, I was sitting on the windowsill in my bedroom looking at what just happened to be the most beautiful night that I could ever remember in Kazimierza Wielka, Poland. There seemed to be millions of twinkling stars lighting up the sky. My window was open and every now and then a gentle, cool breeze washed over me, providing welcome relief from what had been a very hot day. The scent of the flowers from my neighbors' yards and the little garden I had cultivated right below my window was so delightful that I couldn't help but let my mind drift and daydream about my future. Summer was ending, and soon an autumn chill would fill the air. But for now it was just another summer night.

I had just finished my seventh year of school. There wasn't a high school in Kazimierza Wielka and my parents didn't have a lot of money to send me to one out of town, but for some reason I wasn't worried. Instead, I was confident and excited about what my future would hold. Maybe it was because I was a 14-year-old full of hopes and dreams that distracted me from the harsh reality of a war that was inching its way closer and closer to my doorstep – a war that everyone hoped against hope would never touch us.

For me, the path to the future seemed to run through Palestine. I was a passionate and ardent Zionist and was certain that with all the time I had spent with my friends learning about Palestine, and practicing survival skills as part of our club activities, it was a foregone conclusion that I would go there. When my father's brother, my uncle, Menasze Fiszler from Sosnowiec, said he planned to emigrate to Palestine and wanted to take me with him, I thought that would be a terrific personal adventure for me.

On the other hand, I also knew that Palestine wasn't my only option. My mother had a sister, Bella Stein, who lived in New York. She had agreed to sponsor my cousin, Mania Morawiecka, so that she could obtain a visa to emigrate to America. We were expecting those papers to arrive any day. The plan was that after Mania was safely on her way to America, it would be my turn to go, since Aunt Bella promised to sponsor me as well. I let my mind wander about the possibilities America might hold for me. I thought about going to school there, learning English and maybe other languages. I was good at linguistics and I loved to read. Those were precious gifts my mother had passed along to me; she loved to read too.

Palestine or America? Both destinations were so appealing to me and held out such promise for a young man from a small town in Poland. No doubt, it was going to be a difficult decision, but I was so blessed to have such choices in my life. Still, with either choice there were life-altering consequences. What about my life here in Poland? Sure, adventures in faraway places sounded incredible, but I really had such a nice loving family. I suddenly felt a tug in my heart about the prospect of leaving them behind.

At that time, there were eight of us. I shared a home with my three brothers, Mendel, David, and Moshe, my two sisters, Sarah and Leah, my mother, Rachel, and my father, Selig. Our house was filled with so much love that it was hard to imagine life on my own without seeing all of them every day. It would be strange to be so far away, but I shook off my sentimental apprehension. It would be all right, I assured myself, because no matter how far away I roamed, my family would always be there for me. And that night, as I had done on so many nights before, I thanked God for being so lucky to have such a caring and loving family. Just thinking of them made me feel even more certain that my future would blossom before me and that I would always be able to return home to Kazimierza Wielka and to my family.

On August 31, 1939, I went to sleep at about midnight with these wonderful thoughts on my mind. Less than five hours later my world was shattered. What awakened me from my peaceful slumber was the start of the war – a six year nightmare of death and devastation.

The last time I saw my mother, when we were rushing to go into hiding from the Germans, she told me that if I survived the war, I must "Go to America, to my sister, and tell the world what they did to us." I promised her I would. To this day, I continue to keep my word to her, telling the story of my life's journey in classrooms and lecture halls and also on the March of the Living, an annual education program for youth, and now adults, who travel to Poland to learn about Jewish life there before and during WWII, and then go on to Israel to learn about its history and current affairs. In Poland, I share my stories of the Holocaust, and of the labor and concentration camps where so many of my friends, relatives and countrymen were tortured and died. This book continues that journey and mission.

The orchard where my cousin and I spent our summers

Chapter One
Home

I was born Abram Fiszler on February 8, 1925, in Kazimierza Wielka, Poland, a town located between two rivers – the Nidzica and the Małoszówka. Our house was built across from a *błonia* (a park), a free and open playing field for all to enjoy. Across the street, in front of our home, the *błonia* was lined with tall trees, which was a beautiful sight to see and which marked the seasons for us as we waited through the cold winter for signs of warmer weather to come. In the early spring we searched the sky for signs that the storks were returning from their winter hideaways, to build their nests atop the highest tree limbs. We longed to see the first signs of new green shoots sprouting from the bare tree limbs, but in the fall we'd be sad to see the leaves fall and the storks fly away, knowing that summer was about to end. It was a time when life was simple and uncomplicated, and Kazimierza Wielka was an ideal town in which to live.

Our town had a *beit midrash* (a Jewish learning and prayer center), a *mikvah* (ceremonial bath), a kosher butcher, tradesmen, and merchants typical of the towns in my country. Everything we could ever want was there, so there was no need to leave our tight-knit community. Best of all my family was there – not only my parents and my sisters and brothers – but my grandparents, aunts, uncles and cousins as well. We were all very close and looked forward to the times we could gather together – which occurred not just on special occasions, but on almost every weekend.

That is not to say that my childhood in Kazimierza Wielka was always without worry. When I was two years old I swallowed a nail that was a little more than an inch long. The story of how I survived was something my mother told me about when I was old enough to understand. She said that she went to an unlicensed doctor. She could have gone to the town doctor, but she preferred the unlicensed doctor's approach. When she told him my problem, he said, "Look, as long as he sleeps and is not crying, he's not in pain. Watch him. Most probably he swallowed the nail head down and it will come out." After two weeks it came out, but my mother was frantic the whole time waiting for it to happen. Even though I was very young, what I remember about that incident was that everyone was frantically looking around for something, and my mother was hysterical, fearing that I could die. I don't remember anything else. As it turned out, luck was with me.

I guess, however, you could say my good fortune actually began when I was born into a beautiful family. My mother, Rachel, was a wonderful woman who was reserved, understanding and kind. My father, Selig, was also caring and was more gregarious than my mother. All things considered, I would say I inherited my mother's compassionate nature, but I was more like my father in terms of entrepreneurship and business sense.

We kept a kosher home in which Yiddish and Polish were spoken. My mother and father were religious. Even all these years later, I remember my mother lighting candles on Shabbat and on holidays before serving us a wonderful, traditional meal. Holidays were always strictly observed in my home. My mother was a great cook, so even when money was tight, she always made sure we had delicious meals. Her family meant everything to her; she only wanted the best for us. I recall that she would get up early in the morning and work the whole day. Even with six children she did everything herself without any cleaning or cooking help. Yet we never missed a meal, nor did we get sent home from school for wearing dirty or ripped clothing, as did other children. Even though we had no running water in the house, we were always clean.

A few times a day I had to carry drinking water from a general use well. Two pails were attached to a yoke for that purpose, and I had to haul that heavy load through the mud, which sometimes was up to my ankles, because there was no road to and from the well…and that was only part of my water chores. I also had to fetch soft water from the sugar refinery for bathing. Life wasn't always easy, but I felt I had no reason to complain because I came from such a loving home and everyone else also worked very hard. My situation was no different from others around me. When I got up in the morning, one of my first thoughts was of how blessed I was to have such a loving and supportive family. I would start my day with a blessing, thanking God for that.

My mother taught herself to read Polish and Yiddish. How gifted she was! She had such a love of language and words that she used to stay up reading for an hour or two after everyone went to sleep. She especially enjoyed reading the latest chapters of serial stories that ran weekly in the Yiddish newspaper. She couldn't wait to get the latest installment because it was a little treat for her when she could find some time alone. In the same way, I loved reading so much that when we were sent out to play, I used to sneak back home to finish my book. My parents wanted me to go out and play with my friends, but the problem was that if I was reading a good book, I didn't want to stop and go outside. Beyond the world of my books, my home was my refuge.

Our religion was important to our family. My parents wanted to give us an excellent grasp of our faith and heritage. There was no kindergarten, so before I was even old enough to go to public school, my parents arranged for us to have a rich education by hiring Rabbi Yossel who would come to our house to teach us Hebrew and Yiddish subjects. He would sometimes arrive in the dead of winter, and even as a child I used to feel sorry for him because he would shiver from the cold. I remember his beard was often frozen, and his nose was so red it practically glowed. My mother used to give him a glass of warm milk, and as he drank it, he would warm his hands by rubbing them on the glass. It must have felt so soothing because instead of teaching us, he would often fall asleep. My mother used to come and ask me how the lessons were going, and I would say, "Shh, Rabbi Yossel is asleep."

Despite sleeping some of the time, the Rabbi was a good teacher, and when the weather was better, I got a great deal out of being his student. I learned the alphabet, how to read Hebrew, and the *Chumash* (the Five Books of Moses). I was so well-prepared by the Rabbi that by the time I went to public school, at age seven, I was already able to read Hebrew and Polish.

My lessons were not free; my parents paid Rabbi Yossel. Later, when the community engaged a Hebrew instructor to teach modern Hebrew and many other related subjects, families were charged five *zlotys* for each child requiring instruction, which was a lot of money for a middle class family. Although we did not have a lot of money, my parents would do anything to enhance their children's education and lives.

We certainly weren't rich, but we also weren't poor. Although my father struggled to make a living, he was a good provider. He was a businessman who ran a tailoring business rather than actually working as a tailor. Since he had a few people working for him, he didn't have to do much physical work in his factory. It's not that he didn't know how to be a tailor; he was just managing the business so that he could make it more profitable. For instance, he used to cut fabrics for others who would assemble and sew the garments together because he knew how to get the most out of a piece of fabric and a bolt of cloth. This is a special talent for a tailor and a way of keeping costs down. I was surprised that he was able to cut garments freehand, without using a pattern. My father was an entrepreneur. With many other tailors in town he had to be very clever and devise ways to stay one step ahead of his competition. One of the advantages my father had over the others was that he could sometimes have people run the factory for a few days, so that he could go to the wholesalers in Bialystok and Lodz to buy fabrics and sewing supplies. While the other tailors went to the local store to buy their wares retail, my father was able to bypass the middleman and save money for himself and his customers.

Everyone in my town knew my father. He was president of the Jewish community for eleven years, sharing that position with Jozef Rakowski, with whom he had an excellent relationship. Along with their committee, they were responsible for collecting taxes to be used for the upkeep of the Jewish cemetery that our community co-owned with the nearby town of Koszyce. Their responsibilities also included refurbishing the *beit midrash*, which was an old wooden building in great need of repair. Rakowski and my father dreamed of modernizing it, so they worked to have the building fortified and enlarged. It was a huge undertaking for both of them, and when it was finished they took great pride in that achievement. Because of their responsibilities, it was not unusual for my father to come home as late as eleven or twelve at night. As a result, my brothers, sisters and I would lie in our beds waiting for him to come home because he'd always bring us treats – chocolate and candy. Whenever he returned from a business trip he always managed to bring gifts for everyone; he never came back empty-handed. My mother lectured him about it, but she never got upset with him or us. She'd say, "What did you do? You spent money when money is so tight. How can you spend money on chocolate?" But my father would get around her by saying, "No, no, no, I found it in the street," or "Somebody gave it to me," or "I won it in the lottery." He swore he didn't waste any money. I don't think my mother really believed his stories, but she knew he meant well so she couldn't stay mad at him.

When I was seven years old there were six of us. My mother and father provided a loving and safe home for me, my older sister Sarah, who was nine, my younger brother Mendel, who was five, and my younger sister Leah, who was three. My other brothers, David and Moshe, were born later, when we lived in a bigger apartment. I remember that David and Leah looked like my mother, and although our physical traits favored both our parents, emotionally we were all more like our mother. That is not to say that our father was not loving and close to us. It's just that we didn't have the same relationship with him as we did with our mother because he wasn't with us all of the time the way that she was. She was always so busy with our lives that she hardly had time to do anything for herself. When she had free time on a Saturday or Sunday afternoon she would go for long walks in the fields and along the stream at the end of the *błonia*, and even then, she took the younger children with her. My mother was the one who dried our tears, kissed away our bumps and bruises, and went to school to speak to our teachers. I remember that when she came back from school, she would always come home smiling. We did well in school, so she always received good reports about us. We were successful because our parents encouraged us. We loved them so it was important to make them proud of us.

I was seven years old when I started to go to public school from 8 a.m. until 1 p.m., but on days that I had choir practice I was in school until 2 p.m. By 3 p.m. I had to be in Hebrew school, so I would run home, eat something and run off to attend Hebrew classes. By the time I got home from Hebrew school it was 6 p.m., and then I had to eat supper and do my homework for both schools. That left me no time to play. It was no wonder that I looked forward to the weekend when I could be with my friends and kick a soccer ball around or go tobogganing in the winter when there was snow.

For the most part, my very close friends were Jewish and I spent most of my time with them, although I also had quite a few Gentile friends. There was only one school in town which we all attended, but we were not necessarily in the same class. I was in a class with fifty-eight children of whom only two were Jewish, but those numbers changed from year to year. Sometimes there were two, sometimes three, sometimes four Jewish students, but on average I'd say about five percent of the students in each class were Jewish.

We had a long vacation which began at the end of December and ended with the Three Kings celebration, the last official day of Christmas on January 6, which marked the visit of the Wise Men or Magi in the Christian faith. We also had a long break during Easter vacation. Many of my happy childhood memories came from those precious days off from school when we could all play together.

Despite the vacations, keeping up with my hectic school schedule was a real challenge, but I didn't mind. I liked learning and I looked up to my teachers, respecting them as if they were my parents. One of my teachers, Mr. Golenc, would say, "If Abram would put in a little more effort, he could be the first in the class." Of course, he didn't know that when I came home, I had to go to Hebrew school and couldn't really spare any more effort for my school assignments.

I was fortunate in that homework always came easily to me and I never really had to worry and put pressure on myself to complete the coursework that I was assigned. My only problem was when I was asked a question in history or geography; I typically had the right answer but hadn't used the materials that the teacher had assigned to me. I used my own sources of information, and in that way, I hadn't done my homework assignment exactly the way my teacher wanted me to do it. I never failed, however, because I always knew what I was doing. I realized right away that I was more mature than some of my friends. I was better informed and thought "outside the box." That didn't make a difference to them or to me, however.

As was the custom in my hometown, people of the same family or faith lived close to each other. I had between 40 and 50 relatives in my community. Getting together was our form of entertainment. There might be one new movie every two to three months that would come to our town, but the tickets were too expensive for family outings. The best times of my childhood were spent with my aunts, uncles and cousins. We had a large family gathering almost every weekend and would either meet at my house, or most often, we would meet at my maternal grandparents' home on Saturday afternoons, since Sundays were working days. Generally, when all the adults got together, they spent their time eating, talking and telling funny and interesting stories. We didn't go out of town often on holidays because holidays were just another opportunity for all of us to get together, and it was also very expensive to travel. There were eight members of my mother's family -- her parents, five sisters and one brother. My Uncle David and his wife, Balcia, took care of my mother's parents who lived with them. My father, on the other hand, had five brothers and one sister. Although I knew my uncles, aunts and cousins from my father's family, I never got to know my father's parents. I don't recall if they died before I was born or when I was very young.

It was great to be a kid in my family because when we got together, I could run around with about twenty to thirty children around my age. It was a wonderful way to grow up. We'd play with my grandparents' goats. My grandmother would bake batches of cookies and cakes during the week so we could have treats on the weekend. We'd go to the field and play all kinds of games, and at night we'd get flashlights and play hide and seek, staying one step ahead of each other as we ran from one hiding place to another, and even climbed tree tops. The funny thing is that we played in poppy fields, but we didn't know about the effects of poppy in those days. We would pick the poppy seeds and eat them every day. No wonder I was so happy all the time. Who knew? I probably grew up on a high!

As our family continued to grow, my father looked for a place where we could all be more comfortable. A man built a two-story house with five apartments near the sugar refinery. Three apartments were on the ground floor and two were above. The man finished the ground floor with $5,000 that my father had loaned him (about $80,000 in 2014 dollars), but he didn't complete the upper apartments because he ran out of money. Still, that gave us a place to live, since he couldn't pay my father back. Of the three apartments, the landlord gave us the nicest apartment, and then he lived in one and rented the other. That loan enabled my family to live rent-free. It wasn't a spacious place and none of us had a private bedroom. I shared a room with my brothers; my sisters shared another bedroom and my parents had their own room. At the time, it seemed like my father had made a great deal, but in the end he paid a dear price for the business arrangement because he never got any money back. Even though money was owed to him, years later when the Jewish community was liquidated, the deal ended. I never pursued it.

Our beautiful apartment, with its large living room and kitchen, was in a lovely brick building. Because we lived so close to the sugar refinery, we were one of the few families in town that had electricity, and as a result we had lots of company. The Jewish community in my town was like one large family and we were constantly visiting each other. Fortunately, when we moved to this apartment, my Uncle David, his wife and family, and my grandparents, also moved to a place near us. For a while life in our new home seemed ideal.

While living in this apartment, my two youngest brothers were born. Then, there were eight of us: my parents, Sarah, Mendel, Leah, David, Moshe and me. Sarah was sweet and sensitive, and was growing into a lovely young woman with a beautiful voice. Mendel, who was two years younger than me, was quiet and shy. David and Moshe, the two youngest children, were typical little boys, busy with themselves and their group of friends. I was so busy running around with my own friends that I sadly never got to know them as well as I wish I had. Leah, my younger sister, looked just like my mother. She was tall and slim with long legs. She was very graceful and had a beautiful face and the cutest freckles. The one thing that my brothers, sisters and I had in common was that each of us had lots of friends, Jewish and non-Jewish. At that time, it didn't make too much difference if you were Jewish or Gentile – at least that's how it seemed on the surface. But scratch the surface and the differences were there.

One might wonder if we experienced bigotry when we associated with people who were not Jewish. Of course we did. There was no hiding the fact that we were Jewish. Many times there was anti-Semitism, but it was exhibited in subtle ways. In school students would call you a Jew, but it wasn't a big deal. No serious fights resulted. Still, the bigotry was there with some, and somehow we could sense it, but I can't tell you how. When we played soccer we frequently had scuffles, and sometimes at school we got into small fights, but they weren't very serious and no one was ever badly hurt. It was just the kind of schoolyard brawls that boys get into, nothing more than that.

In 1936, I joined a Zionist youth organization called Hashomer Haleumi, which was similar to a scout troop. We operated out of a small room that we rented and decorated with books and paintings. It was the only organization that kept us all busy because we met regularly to learn all that we could about our Jewish history and Hebrew heritage. We were always dreaming about, and planning to, eventually move to Palestine. I also wrote articles for the Hebrew school newspaper, *The Iton*, which served as another outlet for my new-found Zionist zeal.

As members of Hashomer Haleumi, we trained to be tough and resilient. Part of our training was to stay outdoors the whole weekend, which began with our marching three and a half miles from our town to the woods. We would blow a trumpet at five o'clock in the morning as we trooped through different villages, and people would curse us. Dogs barked and people yelled, "What the hell are you doing?" Their reaction amused us. Ordinarily, we didn't want to draw attention to ourselves, but being part of a group made us bold and willing to take some risks. When we got to the woods, we took our "mission" seriously, however. We would look around to make sure there was nothing dangerous in the forest, and just like scouts we would build our own tents and do our own cooking. We'd sing songs, learn about Jewish history, memorize different Hebrew poems, and dance the *hora*. Camping out in the woods was a wonderful childhood adventure and I loved every minute of it. Unfortunately, it didn't happen often enough.

In the summer of 1936, and again in 1937, my cousin Abram (my uncle Josef's son) and I had my father lend us some money so we could rent an orchard in a nearby village, Lolyn. I was only 11 years old and Abram was two years older. We figured out a way to have a great summer vacation and make some spending money for ourselves at the same time. The idea was that at the end of the summer we would pick the fruit from the orchard, sell it, pay my father back, and make some profit. We thought of ourselves as young entrepreneurs. We decided which orchard to rent by visiting different orchards in April when the trees began to bloom. Based on the way the limbs and branches looked, we would estimate how much fruit we could expect to pick. We were pretty good at estimating since we never lost money. I remember those two summers as carefree and fun even though Abram and I had to sleep at the orchard for two months; otherwise the fruit would be stolen. We built our own tent from straw, cooked our own food, and had a German Shepherd for protection. As a matter of fact, it was then that I made scrambled eggs for the first time. I put in so much butter that we both became terribly sick. I thought the more butter I used, the better the eggs would taste. I learned the hard way how to scramble eggs. From then on my cousin did most of the cooking, but I still pitched in.

While I was in the orchard, I spent a lot of time reading whatever newspapers were available. So many things happened in the 1930s that I read about, starting with Hitler coming to power in 1933, followed by the aggressions against, and persecution of the Jews in Germany; the Italian invasion of Abyssinia in 1935; the German occupation of Alsace-Lorraine in 1936; and the events at the 1936 Olympics in Berlin, including the triumph of Jesse Owens, which captivated me. I also read that King Edward gave up the English throne for the woman he loved and I learned about the Spanish Civil War…and I followed American baseball's first Jewish star, Hank Greenberg.

Often, during our summers at the orchard, we had encounters with Polish people who wanted to steal our fruit, but that didn't bother us. We knew how to protect what was ours. Every Friday we would go home to bring back provisions for the following week, and we'd always run into some Polish kids who were waiting to fight us because we were Jewish and they wanted our food. It happened every time, so we expected it. Our only question was how many of them would we have to fight. That didn't deter Abram and me, however, from having two incredible summers that I will always remember.

People sometimes ask me why there was anti-Semitism. In my opinion, it was based on jealousy. The population of Kazimierza Wielka was about 5,000, of which only about 500 were Jews. However, although

Jews made up only about 10 percent of the population, they owned about 80 percent of the businesses in Kazimierza Wielka. That caused resentment. It is as simple as that. The majority of the non-Jewish citizens were farmers, while most of the others worked in the sugar refinery. They had a tough life trying to make a decent living. The farmers worked very hard from early morning until late at night and had to work outdoors in the heat of the summer. Moreover, their livelihood was completely dependent upon the weather conditions. The Jewish people, in contrast, all owned businesses. They were merchants, tailors, shoemakers and bakers who worked hard as well, but it was a different kind of work.

My grandfather was a shoemaker and his son was a shoemaker. My father was a tailor, one of his brothers was a tailor, and two were shoemakers. I remember there were times before the holidays when they worked 24 hours a day. That was nothing unusual, but their hands didn't get dirty the way farmers' hands did. It was not the kind of work like the farmers had to do, tilling their fields in the sweltering heat of the summer, while praying and hoping to have good weather for the harvest. That was the difference.

Despite our differences with our non-Jewish neighbors, we were lucky that until the war broke out we generally got along. Prior to the war, a man named Janek used to come around to make trouble for the Jews. People said he was mentally ill, so we called him Crazy Janek. He had been an officer in the army, but had been dismissed, although we never knew why. When he came into town he never bothered any Poles; only Jews. He used to beat them up whenever he saw them. When a Jew was alone, Crazy Janek would jump him, so older Jews were afraid to walk the streets when he was there. He would come around for a month or two and then disappear. In retrospect, I think Janek acted out the anti-Semitism that others felt but didn't openly express. As I mentioned earlier, there were other ways that bias and bigotry were made clear to us, such as being called a Jew and hearing people say negative things about Jews, but that didn't happen very often.

Anti-Semitism really started to surface a few years before the war, especially after Marshal Józef Piłsudski's death in 1935. He was the leader of the Second Polish Republic who had implemented a "state-assimilation" policy in which citizens were judged not by their ethnicity but by their loyalty to the state. That policy benefited Polish Jews. After his death, prejudices began to surface again. In 1936, Madam Janina Prystorowa, a government official, introduced a bill in Poland's Sejm, the lower house of parliament, to ban the Jewish ritual (kosher) slaughtering of cows. There were so many major problems in the world at that time, including the German threat to Poland, but they spent their time talking about slaughterhouse rules. Why?

It was clear to all of us that that was a way to express anti-Semitism and a way to divide people. They discussed the topic for weeks and weeks even though it was shortly before the outbreak of the war. Instead of taking up the issue of Germany threatening to invade Poland, they wasted time talking about slaughterhouse rituals and stirring up resentment.

To a large extent, the Polish people were in denial about the war. They were being told by the Polish government that the country was safe and they had a false sense of security because of the non-aggression pact Poland had signed with Germany in 1934. We all lived with the hope that there would be no war, but soon the information we received from the outside world told us that we had much to fear. Because we had a radio in our house, people came to listen when Hitler made a speech. It was chilling. I would put on headphones to listen to the radio while people would wait to hear what he said. He screamed so loudly and spoke such formal German that I couldn't understand a lot of it. All I could understand was "Juden, Juden, Juden." That much was unmistakable. Then when I took off the headphones and they asked me what Hitler had said, all I could say was that he said he hates the Jews. The whole speech was full of hate and threats of aggression.

We kept up with the news from Germany when a horrible event captured everyone's attention and had the whole Jewish community talking. A 17-year-old Jew, Herschel Grynszpan (Henry Greenspan), assassinated Nazi Foreign Service Officer, Ernst vom Rath, on November 7, 1938, in Paris. It was terrible. Why would this young man do such a thing? He did it because in October 1938, the Polish Government revoked the passports of all Polish citizens who had lived outside of Poland for more than five years. It was a move calculated to keep Polish Jews from flooding back to Poland after being deported from Germany. Originally, Polish Jews had gone to Germany to make a living during the depression years when unemployment was incredibly high in Poland. When Hitler came to power, however, he ordered the deportation of all Polish Jews, to force them to go back to Poland. Even though they had worked and lived in Germany for many years, paid taxes, and had been welcomed before he came to power, Hitler now insisted that they leave Germany. Hitler deported at least 15,000 Polish Jews residing in Germany, but because Poland had revoked their passports, they were stranded in no man's land. They crossed the German border but couldn't enter Poland. Greenspan's parents were part of that group of exiled Polish Jews, so Greenspan shot the Nazi Foreign Service Officer in Paris to focus the world's attention on their plight.

On Friday nights, because the prayer service was short, we didn't go to the *beit midrash* and instead would gather in groups at the homes of our friends and family and conduct services there. On the Friday following the Greenspan event, my father and I went to a friend's house for the usual Friday night prayers. On that evening, we were at the house of our neighbor, Mendel Salzman. Normally, this would have been a happy occasion. Whenever we assembled as a community on Friday nights, we talked about the week's events and usually people were in great spirits. It was the end of a hard week's work and people expected a good, festive meal after the service. On this evening, however, the mood was different. When I entered the house, everyone was so sad. The tension was so thick it was like someone had just died. I walked in that night not knowing what had happened during the past few days, but it soon became apparent to me that something was terribly wrong. Greenspan's act had cast a pall of fear among the Jewish community that was well founded. While the Germans needed no excuse to attack the Jews, Greenspan's act served as a trigger.

What happened next was horrific. On November 9 and 10, 1938, German mobs attacked Jewish communities throughout Germany, Austria, and in areas of Czechoslovakia that had recently been occupied by the Germans. More than 1,300 synagogues were burned or destroyed; nearly 100 Jews were killed; 30,000 Jews were thrown into concentration camps; 7,000 Jewish businesses were destroyed; and thousands of Jewish homes in Germany were looted and ransacked. This horrible episode was called Kristallnacht (the Night of Broken Glass) because the streets were covered with broken glass from the homes and businesses that were destroyed. From this point forward, Germany intensified its efforts to persecute, and ultimately annihilate, the Jews.

In 1934, Hitler had signed a ten year non-aggression pact with Poland because he was not ready to start a war. He was trying to buy some time to build his war machine. Day after day Germany became stronger. After Germany annexed Austria, and occupied all of Czechoslovakia, Hitler promised the free world that he would not make any more territorial demands. Shortly afterward, however, Hitler gave Poland an ultimatum demanding territorial concessions. Poland refused, insisting Germany was being unreasonable. Stunned by German aggression, Poland signed a pact of mutual assistance with England and France. Everyone involved believed that that would deter Germany from starting a war. As a response to the Polish pact with England and

France, Germany signed a non-aggression pact with Russia. The two dictators, Stalin and Hitler, knew that this was just a meaningless piece of paper. In secret, they agreed to partition Poland. Germany would keep the western part of Poland up to the San River and Russia would occupy the eastern portion of Poland. This agreement would position these two military powers on each side of Poland's border. Hitler wanted to make sure that in case of war, Russia would not intervene. Thus, in August 1939, the stage was set for Hitler's next move.

A little less than a month later, emboldened and unstoppable, the Nazis were on the march to Poland. It was the war we never could let ourselves believe would come to our doorstep. We thought somehow we would be safe in our homes and in our towns. Unfortunately, we soon learned that there was no safe haven for us anywhere.

The barn where I hid with my sister Sarah during the liquidation of our Jewish community in 1942

Chapter Two
The Occupation

On September 1, 1939, Germany attacked Poland without any warning. Poland had been asked by its allies not to mobilize because they didn't want to antagonize Hitler. As a result, Poland was completely unprepared for Germany's invasion, which was swift and unrelenting. We were at war.

I was awakened at about 4:30 a.m. by the incredible roar of low flying planes. I remember the planes were so low that I could see the pilots! To my horror, I saw swastikas on the planes' wings. I knew immediately that we were at war; the war we each feared and worried about was here. My first reaction was not to cower in fear, but to get dressed quickly and join the people I saw gathering in the streets. Dazed and horrified, my neighbors huddled around any radio they could find. They strained to listen to understand the extent of what was happening to their sleepy little town and their country. I listened as well, but the airways were filled with what sounded like gibberish, which were actually codes for the Polish Army. Stunned, we all started to react as a community. We could not wait for our country to tell us what to do, so we did what little we could to take care of ourselves, hoping that our army, which we thought was formidable, would protect us. We covered our windows to make sure that no lights would attract airplanes. We waited out the assault, hoping in vain that every lull in the action meant that the attack was over.

I could clearly hear the sounds of anti-aircraft artillery stationed outside Krakow, which was about 35 miles away. I could also hear the sound of exploding bombs in the surrounding area. We all felt terrible. But as bad as it was that night, I could not have imagined what was to come next for my family, my community and the rest of the world.

The Jewish people, not aware of the unholy alliance between Germany and Russia, lived under the false belief that in the event of war, Poland could and would defend itself. As Jews, we had much to fear. We had been told that the Polish army was the second strongest in Europe and we believed it. Only France was stronger at that time. We could not possibly imagine how strong and how well prepared Germany was for war. Its army, navy and air force unleashed a blitzkrieg. There was no power in the world that could have stopped them at that time. Perhaps the combined forces of England and France could have been effective, but those countries were very opposed to war because of their citizens' memories of the horrors of World War I.

Unfortunately, by the third day of the war, masses of civilians were running to the East to escape the advancing, overpowering German army. We hoped that the Polish army was retreating to more defensible lines like the Vistula or Bug Rivers, but, as we found out, all our hopes were unfounded. While Germany was destroying the Polish army, the Russian army occupied eastern Poland. At the same time, England and France declared war on Germany, as was outlined in the treaty, but other than declaring war, England and France did nothing to stop the German and Russian aggression. We Jews were trapped!

On the seventh day of the war, a Polish Carpathian Cavalry Division arrived in our town. As a curious teenager, I went to the *błonia* to talk to some of the soldiers. I was anxious to learn what was happening. At about lunchtime, much to my surprise, all hell broke loose. Suddenly there was gunfire that sounded like it was coming from all directions at once. I ran home while bullets whistled around me. I was very lucky not to have been killed. As I entered my home, I found it filled with friends and neighbors, seeking safety and protection from the battle. Part of the town was burning, and because our home was brick, it was considered a safe haven. The battle lasted until the early evening, when the Polish army retreated, leaving behind their cache of armaments scattered everywhere.

It wasn't until the next morning that it seemed safe to take a walk to find out what was happening. It was a horrible sight. The battlefield, filled with the anguished cries of the wounded and the scent of death, had come to the streets of my town. Some of my teachers were trying to tend to the wounded Polish soldiers who were strewn all over the fields. I joined them. The wounded were in dire shape, having been left in the fields unattended throughout the night. While the German casualties were taken away by ambulances, the Poles were left to suffer. As we carried them on stretchers, they kept asking, "How far is the hospital?" Regretfully, we had to tell them that our doctors could only administer first aid, but that they would be taken to a hospital in Krakow, which as stated earlier, was about 35 miles away.

The following morning a German soldier came to our home and ordered all adult males to gather on a field adjacent to the cemetery, to bury the horses that had been killed in the battle. Because of their weight and size, we had to use chains to gather all the horses in one place. The day was very hot, making this onerous task even more difficult. The Germans supplied us with vodka because of the overwhelming stench of decaying flesh. Our Rabbi Unger, who had never done any manual labor, begged me to help him. If the Germans noticed that he was not working as hard as the others, he would be severely punished. I was only 14 years old, but I did as much as I was capable of doing to compensate for his inability to do much physical labor.

The Germans destroyed our *beit midrash* on the first day of occupation. Years later I learned from an eyewitness that Polish citizens dug under the destroyed building to search for treasure they believed we Jews had hidden there. Some of those people were our neighbors and friends…or so we had thought.

From then on, laws pertaining to Jews were passed daily. We had to wear yellow star armbands. We were not allowed to go to school. We had to abide by a curfew. We had to supply manpower for forced labor, which consisted of working in our town's sugar refinery. We shoveled snow. We washed German vehicles and moved heavy furniture and heavy safes in the building taken over by the German governor. Many times when I returned home, tired and beaten from a brutal day's work, my mother was waiting for me with a hug and kiss, and a warm meal. My mother was able to make the intolerable tolerable for me.

In our town the occupation force consisted of a German Governor, Herr Schmidt, who had an Austrian assistant, and a German civilian administration. We also had German police. The existing Polish police retained their original responsibilities, but now they reported to the German administration. Additionally, the town had twelve Ukrainian guards who worked for the Germans in the sugar refinery. The Ukrainians volunteered to work for the Germans because they were promised that the Ukraine would become independent from Poland and Russia if the Germans were victorious. My father volunteered to make his tailoring factory available to the Germans and Ukrainians, thinking that this effort to build good working relations would help the Jewish community. At that time, there were many rumors about Ukrainian atrocities targeting Jews – which later proved to be true – but my father and I had good relations with the twelve Ukrainian guards in our town. In fact, one of them, Stasuk, even taught me how to play chess.

My father's position as head of the Jewish community was becoming more and more difficult with each passing day. Many Jewish men had to travel out of town to make a living, but were not allowed to do so without a special permit. My father had to obtain these permits from the governor, but only received a fraction of what was needed. Despite all the pleas for additional permits, there were none, creating hardships for many families. During this period my father would bring home strangers that could not travel after the curfew. I recall one night I woke up and saw a body on my bedroom floor. I thought it was my mother, since she usually was the last one to go to bed, and I let out a blood-curdling scream.

Because of the constant pressure and demands, my father became very ill. A doctor from a neighboring town arrived by sled to treat him. Miraculously, my father made a complete recovery, but he never recovered from the guilt of knowing that he could not help everyone. That was just one of the many difficult challenges my father faced.

In the middle of 1941, I became a policeman for the Jewish community because of my father's influence, and was excused from forced labor. I was just 16 years old, and while not having to do forced labor was a benefit, my father also thought it would give our family a better chance to survive. He had heard that in many towns during 1941-1942, the families of Jewish policemen were left intact while others were taken away. There were rumors that some of the Jewish police in other towns abused their power, but that was not true in my town where the police's primary task was to supply men for forced labor. Unfortunately, being a policeman singled us out for trouble from an unwelcome return visitor to our town.

Crazy Janek had disappeared before the outbreak of the war. We had not seen nor heard from him for more than a year. Suddenly he reappeared, however, causing distress for all of us Jews, especially those who were most vulnerable. He seemed to get some sick satisfaction from pulling the beards of the older men and beating them up. Soon, Janek became emboldened and started coming after the Jewish police in the town.

There were three shifts at the sugar refinery. One of the shifts changed at midnight. Because of the curfew, that shift had a Jewish police escort. After dropping off the men, Janek would jump the policeman and beat him up. One day after I dropped off a group of laborers, Janek jumped me. Being prepared, I struck him with a stick and then ran away. The next morning when I looked out my bedroom window, I saw two men fighting in the street. Janek was beating up my friend, Kalman Dula. I ran out barefoot, in my shirt and shorts, and grabbed Janek's hand. Before I was able to do anything, someone speaking perfect German, grabbed my hand and warned me not to interfere. I realized that I was surrounded by hostile people who were encouraging Janek. Making my way through the crowd, I ran to the German police station for help. I suspected that if I had gone to the Polish police for help, they would not have intervened. When I arrived at the German police station I met a German gendarme, Master King, who had always been very kind to me. I do not know why he treated me well, but perhaps it was because I was young, or perhaps I reminded him of his own children. I told him that Janek was interfering with our duty to accompany laborers to the sugar refinery. Unfortunately, Master King could not do anything because he was manning the station by himself at that time. He did, however, call the Polish police and asked for their assistance, but that presented a new problem for me because of the distance between the German and Polish police stations. I was afraid, but I took a chance and went to the Polish police station anyway. In the interim, Janek went into hiding.

When I arrived at the station, the commander there informed me that he, too, was all alone on duty, but he called the school where the police were assisting Polish farmers delivering grain to the Germans. One of the Polish officers I had gotten to know was assigned to help me. Fortunately, some kids told us where Janek was hiding and soon afterward, Janek was arrested. He was taken away and we never heard from him again.

Despite everything that was happening, life went on in Kazimierza Wielka. Couples fell in love, married and had babies. My sister Sarah fell in love with a young man named Moniek Singer, who was from the neighboring town of Proszowice. She met Moniek when she went on a business trip to Krakow with my father. They stayed in a hotel in which their room was so full of cockroaches, they never went to sleep. Instead, they went to the lobby along with everyone else in the hotel, and there she met my future brother-in-law.

It was clear that my father was pleased that Sarah had met such a nice fellow. She couldn't wait to get home to tell us all about him, and just a few days later Moniek visited and stayed with us. We all got along very well. He was a good-looking, pampered, only son from a well-to-do family. He was an intelligent, elegant, well-dressed and well-mannered man, and those qualities really impressed my mother. I can understand why Moniek fell deeply in love with my sister almost at first sight, because she was a wonderful person. She was talented, smart and beautiful, as well as a very good cook. Moniek became a frequent guest in our home, and my mother really fell in love with him too.

However, Moniek's visit one April morning in 1942, was anything but his usual social call. I remember how disheveled and breathless he was when I saw him standing in our doorway. He had run the fifteen miles from his town to tell us that there was a liquidation of the Jews in Proszowice. He ran away, but not before his mother was taken away on a transport. He asked if we could possibly do something to find her because my father, as head of the Jewish community, had contacts with the Germans. He was hoping against hope that my father could use his influence to get his mother released. Poor Moniek had no idea where else to go for help, and he knew that there was almost no chance that we or anyone else could save her.

The problem with finding Moniek's mother was that we didn't know where they took her. We went to the Jewish community center, in Mr. Rakowski's home, and discovered that there was a telegram from the town of Slomniki, about 25 miles away, in which they pleaded for us to bring food for the people that had been brought there from different towns and villages that had been liquidated. We thought that must be where Moniek's mother was. It all made sense.

We had our Jewish bakers bake a few hundred loaves of bread. Next someone was needed to bring the bread to Slomniki, so Kalman Dula and I volunteered to go, hoping to find out about Moniek's mother. That was my first encounter with just how dangerous the Nazis were. Before that, there were rumors about what they were doing to Jews, but now we saw it with our own eyes.

I will never forget the scene when we arrived in Slomniki. It was a very hot day and Kalman and I made our way to the large field where we saw about 10,000 Jews gathered like sardines under the burning sun. Ukrainian soldiers who had served as guards for the transports were marching up and down the soccer field carrying weapons – shovels, axes and sledgehammers – on their shoulders. We saw the head of the Jewish police, David Bialobroda, and approached him and asked if he could help us get Moniek's mother out of there. He said that since she was an older woman it would be impossible. The only option would be to sneak her out in an empty water barrel, and that would be unmanageable for her. We had to give up the idea and leave, fearing for our own lives. I remember feeling so helpless as I listened to many of those poor souls screaming "water, water." Their anguished cries haunted me after I left Slomniki that day. They haunt me still.

On the way back, Kalman and I were so distraught, exhausted and repulsed by what we had seen, that we stopped at a Polish farm to buy some homemade potato vodka. It was so bad that we became very ill. As soon as we arrived back in Kazimierza Wielka, we went to the community center where we found all the leaders of the Jewish community, including my father, celebrating. The contrast between the joy in that room, and the scenes we had just witnessed in Slomniki made me faint.

When I regained consciousness, I asked my father why everyone was celebrating. He said that the German governor had promised that no action would be taken against our community for six months. I couldn't believe it. Six months was no time at all and there was no sign that the war would end soon. How could we celebrate when we had just seen what was ahead for us in six months' time? It was horrifying to me. I saw our future in Moniek's face when I told him that we could not save his mother. When we had left, he knew there was almost no chance that we would be able to, but facing the reality of it hit him hard. Moniek didn't return to Proszowice and instead stayed with my family for a brief time. He grew very close to my mother as he dealt with his terrible loss, before he relocated to the Krakow ghetto.

The Nazis were very shrewd. They had a systematic way of organizing the destruction of the Jews. The event in Proszowice was the first action that the Germans took against the Jews in our area. Beginning in 1942 they started to take Jews away from certain towns, but they took care not to remove all the Jews at once. They would take away fifty or sixty percent, while the remaining Jews went into hiding. Some who went into hiding felt that once the fifty or sixty percent were taken away, they would be able to return and resume life as before. It was a false sense of security because eventually the Germans would come back to take them all, but there was always the hope that perhaps by the time the Germans came back, the war would be over.

In Kazimierza Wielka, what the governor had said was true. It took six months before the catastrophe hit us and neighboring towns. But that didn't mean that those last six months were without danger. A Polish police officer and his wife had committed suicide. The Nazis accused the Polish underground partisans of murdering them and the Germans surrounded Kazimierza Wielka with machine guns and canisters of gasoline. The medical examiner performed an autopsy, and the Germans said that if they found that the couple had been murdered, they would destroy the whole town. To that end, the Germans took hostages and my father worried that he would become one of them. He was smart enough, however, to hide in the basement of the police station, and luckily, for some reason, they never looked there.

After two days the autopsy was completed and the medical examiner declared that the couple had committed suicide so the town was safe – for the moment. We came so close to a disastrous end....and after the war I learned that the couple was, indeed, murdered.

As the promised six months raced by, we grew increasingly worried about the eventuality that we too were going to be liquidated. Everyone, including the Jewish police, was vigilant to see if there were any signs or changes in the Germans' behavior. The Germans overran Proszowice so quickly and without warning that we wanted to be prepared. However, we realized there was not much that we could do. Horrifying stories began to circulate through our community with alarming frequency, about atrocities being committed at Treblinka, Auschwitz and other concentration camps, but we didn't want to believe them. After all, no one with a clear mind could imagine such unbelievable events or anticipate what was going to happen next.

We tried everything to save ourselves. From the beginning of the German occupation, our occupiers, especially the governor and his assistant, were bribed with money and jewelry donated by the Jewish congregation. One of the most difficult tasks that my father and Mr. Rakowski faced was determining which Germans could be bribed to buy us some temporary safety and security. You risked your life if you tried to bribe someone and you picked the wrong person.

In April 1942, my father sent me to Miechow, the state capital, with a bundle of jewelry to bribe officials hoping they'd leave us alone. I gave that bribe to the president of the Jewish ghetto, who was our contact.

When I arrived people were in mourning because something terrible had just happened. Whatever it was had people so upset that they were afraid to leave their homes. Later I learned that a Jewish policeman, who was to have been married in a nearby town, arrived at the train station after Sabbath. Even though he had permission to travel by train after curfew, a drunk German at the station shot and killed him. The bride's family and guests were waiting for him to arrive in the next town, but he never did. The ghetto population was devastated because he was one of the most well-liked policemen in the ghetto.

In another bribery situation, I was sent to Proszowice to see, Mr. Pinczewski, the president of the Jewish community, who was also our contact. I was sent there with jewelry to bribe a German with whom he did "business." I was very pleased to meet Pinczewski and his family. We had dinner and then I left the jewelry with him, hoping for the best. A few weeks after my visit, however, I heard rumors that something terrible had happened to Pinczewski and his family. I didn't find out what happened until after the war, when I learned that one day two black Mercedes parked in front of Pinczewski's home. A Gestapo officer and Bialobroda stepped out of the car and told Pinczewski, his wife and five sons to come out of their home. Pinczewski was asked to give the Gestapo officer the jewelry hidden in his home. Pinczewski, insisting that he had none, received a terrible beating. It must have seemed strange to Pinczewski because the high ranking Gestapo officer who was beating him had been bribed by him many times before.

The officer knew Pinczewski's family and realized the man's fifth son was not there. The Germans ransacked the whole house and finding nothing told the soldiers to look for the missing son. The young man was visiting his girlfriend. When he found out that they were looking for him, he decided to go home. His girlfriend tried to talk him out of it, but since he knew his father had good connections with the Germans, he was not afraid. When he got close to home, however, he saw his family being held at gunpoint and knew something was wrong. Unfortunately, he had already been spotted by the Germans and couldn't turn and run. He was shot along with his entire family, on orders from the high-ranking Gestapo officer who had been bribed by Pinczewski before. That brutal officer either acted out of self-interest because he had taken too many bribes and Pinczewski knew too much, or he acted out of hatred. Who knows?

Even with all the risks that came with paying off Germans for our very survival, bribes were one of the only means we had to stay on their good side. When Moniek fled from the liquidation in his town, he left a considerable amount of jewelry behind so I went to Proszowice and broke into his abandoned house. I took as much jewelry and valuables as I could find and safely carry to return to him, instead of leaving them behind for looting Germans or Poles. On the train going home I recognized some people that I knew well enough to suspect that they were collaborating with the Germans. Instead of ignoring them, I went over to them and offered to light their cigarettes and talked with them all the way home. Luckily they were not suspicious of my actions and no one looked in my suitcase.

Back home, my father was doing his best to make sure that life in the community was as normal as possible. He knew that bribes eventually wouldn't work anymore and that the Jewish community would be liquidated. It was inevitable, but my father never gave up trying to keep the community together. He was able to get an unofficial permit for religious services, which were held in my grandfather's home as well as in other residences. The governor agreed to let us have prayer meetings, but he wouldn't commit to that on paper, so it was an unwritten understanding that my father had with him. My father, however, always wanted to be out in the open about that because he did not want the Germans to be surprised if they found out we were holding services without a written permit.

I recall that on the last Yom Kippur before the liquidation of our Jewish community, we were *davening* (praying), when our lookouts came running in to inform us that the Germans were coming down the street. We closed the doors. My father went outside to speak to the German soldiers. To this day, I have no idea what he said to them, but they didn't interfere. The bravery and courage my father showed that afternoon made me proud and frightened at the same time. Unfortunately, that was my father's last good deed for the congregation. Shortly afterward, the Jewish community was liquidated.

On Thursday, October 1, 1942, at about 10 p.m. there was a knock on our door. The German governor told my father, "I've helped you until now but there's an order that all the Jews in this town will be liquidated. There is nothing I can do to help you. The orders come from my superiors and I am helpless. I cannot do anything for you. Save yourself. Do whatever you can." He told us not to tell anyone, but we let everyone know what was going to happen. From that time on, people were crying and saying their goodbyes. I still don't think they could truly comprehend the hopelessness and severity of the situation. There was no time to think realistically. Everyone began frantically looking for someplace to hide. That went on all day Friday, Saturday and Sunday. It is impossible to describe those few days. By Sunday everyone was running in all directions because Monday the liquidation was to take place. There really aren't any words that can describe how terrifying and traumatic that experience was.

When the order came that Kazimierza Wielka would be liquidated, all we could hope for was a miracle that I knew would never happen. I had seen too much to think otherwise. Memories of trying to rescue Moniek's mother from Slomniki were all the evidence I needed as to how dire this situation was. My family decided to hide. We gave lip service to the notion that perhaps the Germans would take others and leave so that we would be able to come out of hiding after that. There was a flicker of hope that we were still dealing with a civilized enemy. No one wanted to think of the worst, but from the time that the governor came and told my father the liquidation was about to begin, that flickering hope began to die.

We had to come up with a plan. Where would the eight of us hide? I had befriended a Polish girl, Izia Rutkowska, whom I had a crush on. My parents were not too happy about this because she was Gentile, but we were just good friends from school. Her family was kind and took a liking to me. I was as comfortable in their home as I was in any of my Jewish friends' homes. There was even a time when they invited me over for a meal. It was delicious but non-kosher, and I felt guilty eating it. I felt like I was doing something wrong the entire time I was there, but I didn't say anything. An additional reason I felt comfortable in their home was that Roman Sikorski, Izia's uncle, was my father's business friend.

Mr. Sikorski was much older than me, probably about my father's age. I used to spend hours with him discussing politics. He entrusted me with the underground newspaper after the war began, even though if I had been caught with that paper, I would have been killed and the whole town would have been destroyed. It was because of our friendship, that when the threat of the Jewish liquidation came to my town, I asked Mr. Sikorski if he could hide my sister Sarah and me. Fortunately, he said he would. It was impossible to find a hiding place for all of my family together, so we had to split up. Despite the risk to their own lives, Mr. Sikorski and his family, including his aunt, Mrs. Niewiadomska, turned out to be one of the families that did their best to help and protect the Jews.

As we made preparations to leave, I remember my mother, always the nurturer, making packages for everyone with food and other things we would need, the night we said goodbye to each other. We tried to remain calm, but when my youngest brother Moshe, who was seven years old, came to me and asked me to help him put on a tie, I yelled at him and said it was not a wedding. I feel so badly that that was the last thing we talked about. It still haunts me. At least I remember that the last thing I did before I left the house was kiss and hug him goodbye. I'd like to believe that on his last night on earth he was thinking about that hug and kiss rather than being shouted at by his older brother. I'll never know.

My mother hid in a neighbor's barn with Leah, David and Moshe. My father also had to find hiding places for my mother's two sisters and their families, so he decided to hide them in the same barn with my mother. Although it was risky hiding so many people in one place, time was short and there were few options. He also knew that my mother would take some comfort knowing that her sisters were with her, but it would be too risky for him to stay there as well. My father and my brother, Mendel, then found separate hiding places.

We were so naïve, we couldn't conceive of the danger we were facing. After the 9 p.m. curfew on Sunday night, those who hadn't gone into hiding were not allowed to be outside. After I got my sister settled in Mr. Sikorski's barn, I did what I could to help others to their hiding places. Even though I had a permit, it was still very dangerous. I took a big risk, but somehow I wasn't stopped. At about 10:30 p.m., I joined Sarah. All we could do then was wait and pray that we would be spared.

It was a bitter cold October evening, with Sarah and me freezing as we waited out the night in the Sikorski's barn. The ominous silence was interrupted by rustling in the eaves. Sarah asked what the noises were because she was afraid. I knew they came from rats or mice, but I told her that Mr. Sikorski was breeding pigeons. I was trying so hard to keep Sarah from being frightened, so I wanted to reassure her and keep her calm. I also knew there was far more to be scared of outside the barn than inside.

We didn't sleep that night. At daybreak we heard gunshots. There was no mistaking it now; we knew that the liquidation had begun. I didn't know where the shots were coming from or how many people were being killed. The shooting went on for many, many hours. All we could do was wait, not speak nor move, fearful that the slightest sound would alert someone who might alert the Germans and betray our hiding place.

My grandfather, now a widower, was still living with my Uncle David and Aunt Balcia. As the Germans began liquidating his neighborhood, they tried to take him outside. He resisted. I was told that he said, "I'm not going anywhere. I have been in this house all these years and I'm not leaving." The Germans shot him immediately. When I learned this, I realized that the gunfire we heard when the liquidation began included the shots that killed my grandfather whom I loved so much.

My grandfather was only the first of many people dear to me that would be killed in the Nazi's zeal to wipe the Jews off the face of the earth. Another one of them was my cousin Yosef, who played in a sports group called the Nidzica Soccer Club. He was five or six years older than me, and oh how I idolized him. He was good looking, smart and athletic; I wanted to be just like him. More than that, Yosef was a wonderful, caring and kind human being; a credit to his family. Yosef always made time to come by on Sundays and teach all of us how to play soccer. Sadly, I never found out the circumstances surrounding his death. You could say he was just another casualty of the liquidation, but not to me. I adored him and his senseless death sickened me.

My grandmother had died from natural causes during the first year of the war, when she was 70 years old. It was a crushing blow to us, but the tragedies in my family really started when my mother's only brother died in the late 1930s. I don't know exactly what happened to him. He was taken to a hospital in Krakow with pneumonia, but because he had moved to where his wife's family lived, we didn't know much more than that. My mother visited him often in the hospital before he died. He was a terrific guy who was smart and athletic. It was a terrible blow when we learned that he had died, because he was only in his 30s. I admired him and was so proud of him. Following his death, I was so sad and the world seemed empty without him. I was so angry at God for taking him away, but when the killing began I realized he was lucky. And the same could be said for my grandmother, who was a very religious person. Maybe God saved both of them from all of the horror and granted them the chance to die in peace.

That long October night I didn't think about the gift God had given my grandmother and my favorite uncle. My mind was on the living. I counted the hours hoping that it was truly darkest before the dawn and that our family would reunite from our hiding places and would find a way to remain together and survive. But when the morning came, nothing had changed. Sarah and I were still hiding in an attic in a barn between the roof and platform, cut off from the rest of the world. I felt so helpless. I wanted so much to know what was going on outside. Mr. Sikorski came by a few times and I asked him to tell me what was happening. Then Mr. Sikorski stopped coming to speak to us. The following day he came in and I was frantic to know what was going on. I said, "You must tell me the truth. I know you are avoiding me. What happened to my family?" He responded, "Your mother, two brothers and your sister were caught. They were all taken away with the transport." I was stunned to learn that in one day Leah, David, Moshe and my mother were gone, and I had no idea if my brother, Mendel, and my father were safe.

Years later I was told by my friend, Izia, that she saw the transport pass in front of the barn where Sarah and I were hiding. She saw my mother break down in tears knowing that Sarah and I were there. Izia said my mother was the only one who was crying. Imagine how horrible it was for her. When she passed by she knew we were there and she would never see us again. Had I known that she was in the transport passing in front of our hiding place I would have joined her. I realize now that if I had done that I would not have lived to write this story, but I never would have let her be alone. That night Sarah and I cried all night, our grief mixing with our terror and fear that we would be the next to be found and killed. We didn't know what to do. I tried to comfort my sister, and I also knew I had to find a way to save her and myself. I also had to find out what happened to my father and my brother, Mendel.

More than anything, my mother's last words to me when we parted kept coming back to me. "If you should survive, go to America to my sister. Then tell the world what they did to us." It's almost as if she somehow knew I would be the one to survive. Now I knew I had to do what my mother asked me to do, but first, I had to stay alive, and Sarah and I had to get out of Kazimierza Wielka before the Germans found us.

It was at 13 Miodowa Street, Krakow that
I tried to get forged papers to escape the Nazis

Chapter Three
Then We Were Four

With our mother, David, Moshe and Leah, having been taken away on a transport, the situation was very bleak. Sarah and I had no idea what to do next. When we heard from Mr. Sikorski that our brother, Mendel, had come to find out about us, we were somewhat consoled, knowing that at least he was alive. Mendel didn't know that we were hiding in Mr. Sikorski's barn, but thought that Mr. Sikorski might know something about us. Mr. Sikorski, however, was reluctant to say too much to him, fearing that if the Germans caught Mendel and tortured him he would reveal where we were. The Nazis made no secret of the fact that they would shoot the entire family of anyone who dared to hide Jews. Mr. Sikorski had already taken a tremendous risk by hiding us. He was endangering the lives of his whole family – his wife, Lola, his daughter, Musia, his niece, Izia, and his aunt, Mrs. Niewiadomska – and himself. How kind, brave and noble he was. He couldn't be expected to do more.

When we heard that my father had also come to ask about us, Sarah and I were thankful that he too was alive, but now we were very concerned for both him and Mendel. Unlike Mendel, my father knew that we were with Mr. Sikorski, but he couldn't talk to us for fear that someone might notice and reveal our hiding place. Sadly, there were too many people in town that couldn't be trusted.

The Germans were angry that so many Jews had gone into hiding. Out of the 600 Jews now living in town (100 or so having come from other towns), they caught or killed 180 to 190. It was an embarrassment to them that they couldn't report that all the Jews had been liquidated, so they devised a plan. The Germans posted signs all over town asking for the Jews to come out of their hiding places voluntarily. They promised that they would be saved and taken to a labor camp where they would be given shelter and food until the end of the war. As a result, more than 300 Jews came out of their hiding places. The Germans assembled them on the third floor of the school, where they were locked up at night but were allowed to roam freely, in the town, during the day. By giving them freedom during the day, the Germans believed that they would be the bait to lure more people out of their hiding places. My brother was in the school with the others, but my father wouldn't go there. Instead, he came out at night to learn what was happening, and during the day went back to his own hiding place in Odonow, a nearby village. It was very dangerous for my father to come out at night, and to this day, I don't know how he was able to do it, but he did.

After a week, I realized my sister would not be able to take hiding in the barn much longer. We were hiding in such a small space, afraid to move or make a sound. We were scared that we might be caught and Sarah could not cope with our living arrangements and the horror of everything that was going on around us. Mr. Sikorski and I agreed that it was time to send Sarah to the ghetto in Krakow, where Moniek, Sarah's boyfriend, was already. Mr. Sikorski told me he would accompany Sarah there so it wouldn't be so obvious that she was Jewish and wouldn't be recognized so quickly. Once again, this courageous man took an enormous risk for us.

So, after a week in hiding, I said goodbye to my sister. She left with Mr. Sikorski for Krakow. While waiting for Mr. Sikorski to return, it seemed like the day would never end. I imagined all kinds of terrible things happening to them.

The following morning, however, Mr. Sikorski returned and informed me that Sarah had arrived safely in Krakow and was with Moniek in the ghetto. I was so relieved. It was a small victory, but in this time of deep despair, it was enough. One of us was taken care of, but what would become of my father, my brother and me? I couldn't stay hiding in Mr. Sikorski's barn forever. Each day I lived with the threat of being caught and killed.

My brother was still looking for me. I was afraid that if Mr. Sikorski didn't tell him where I was he would be shot while roaming the streets. I couldn't let that happen; I had to do something before it was too late. I asked Mr. Sikorski to tell Mendel not to go back to the school because I didn't trust the Germans. He had to find another hiding place for a few days until he heard from me again. Luckily, our landlady, Mrs. Jendrawska, offered to hide him. Not going back to the school saved Mendel's life. More than a week after the liquidation began, the Germans took the 324 Jews from the school and told them they were being transported to the train station to be relocated from there. They were taken by horses and buggies, driven by Poles whom the Germans had coerced. The next day, Mr. Sikorski told me the most basic details about what had happened. All I knew was that at one point the road split, and instead of going to the station, each horse and buggy turned off the road into the woods. There, the Jews were ordered to undress and 15 people at a time were taken to be shot. Years later I came face to face with one of the poor souls who had to drive some of those people to their deaths.

In 2004, I worked with three boys from Rockville Centre, N.Y. who were preparing for their Bar Mitzvahs. Each had decided to work on a Holocaust-related project as part of their community service. I met with them (Luke, Michael and Zach) weekly to teach them the history of the Holocaust, focusing on my personal history. During that period, I got to know the boys and their families so well that we jokingly said, perhaps we could all go to Poland together so that they could walk in my footsteps. In the summer of 2007, all three boys went to Spain to study Spanish. Their parents planned to meet them there, and when planning their trip, their mothers approached me wondering if, in fact, I would meet them in Poland, since they were already going to be in Europe. Not only did I meet the boys and their parents in Warsaw, but I was joined by my wife, Rhoda. We hired a guide who transported us during seven transformative days, touring Warsaw, Krakow, Plaszow, Auschwitz and my hometown of Kazimierza Wielka. While visiting my former school, I was approached by an elderly Polish man who felt compelled to share his story with me. It was a cold, rainy day and he had been waiting outside the school eager to clear his conscience. He informed me that when he was a young man the Germans forced him to take his horse and wagon, which held Jewish men, women and children, to the station. However, at a certain point, where the road divided, all the drivers were forced to take them to the forest where they were murdered. That was the first time that this man had revealed what he had done. When he heard that a survivor had returned to Kazimierza Wielka, he felt that he had to share this ugly event. He had been carrying it on his conscience for all those years. The boys and their parents were stunned, when after hearing his story, I gave that poor soul some money because I felt sorry for him.

I shudder to think about the fate of the people murdered that day. Can anyone imagine how those people felt? How terrified they must have been waiting for their turn to be shot. Meeting that man brought back memories of that awful day…and I also remembered that those woods were the same beautiful woods that I had played in as a child.

The Slonowice woods were a beautiful place, where we would picnic as kids. On Saturday afternoons I would lie in the grass and just stare up at the trees that seemed to reach the sky. It was so lovely and usually so silent. All I could hear was the sound of the birds… Now I can never think of those woods the same way again. I never would have imagined that such a place would become a burial site for so many of my relatives and friends. After the war, a monument was built there in memory of those who had been murdered, but unfortunately that monument was destroyed by vandals and later was replaced with just a cold slab.

Once Mr. Sikorski told me what had happened to those poor people, I knew I had to act. It was too dangerous to remain in hiding. I waited a few days for things to cool off and as a result, my brother stayed with our landlady a few days longer than expected. Finally, after more than two weeks in hiding I contacted my brother through Mr. Sikorski, telling him to meet me at a small train station in Odonow, outside our town, so we could catch the 6 a.m. train to Krakow. I didn't want to meet him at the main train station in Kazimierza Wielka because there were always Germans there looking for Jews. Now there was no turning back for my brother or me.

On Thursday night I went to Mrs. Niewiadomska's apartment to bathe and get cleaned up. I also shaved, leaving a slight moustache. I put on a heavy coat and hat so that my face was almost covered. It was time to begin my treacherous journey. At about 4 a.m., I left the house. Mrs. Niewiadomska walked me to the gate, embraced me and cried. She said, "I'm going back to a warm bed and you're going out into the cold unknown." She blessed me and said, "May God watch over you." I walked like a fugitive going from the shadows of one house to the next, afraid of informers as I made my way to the station. With a heavy heart I walked by our home, where not long ago there had been so much life, joy and happiness, but now was quiet and dark. My little garden had been trampled… everything gone forever.

Mr. Sikorski went with me to the train station, but he didn't want me to walk with him. He worried that if we were caught, he would be shot, too, so he walked about 50 feet behind me. In order to get to the train station I had to walk close to the German police station. Near the sugar refinery I crossed the street and disappeared into the darkness of the dense tall trees in the park. Mr. Sikorski was still behind me when he was stopped by the German police. I didn't dare stop to see what happened. I had to trust that he could talk his way out of trouble. If I had been walking with him, or if I had left the house two to three minutes later, I would not be here. When he was stopped, his papers were checked and they let him go, but he never made the train.

Once I got close to the station, I felt my heart racing. I thought I had a good plan but all the pieces needed to fall into place: Mendel and I would go to Krakow together and would try to find Moniek in the ghetto. We thought Moniek would be able to help us. Before he had left for the ghetto, Moniek gave me an address in Krakow - 13 Miodowa Street. It was a restaurant in the middle of town where he told me he would meet us, and we could get forged papers stating we were Gentile.

Because there was a blackout, everything was dark in the station. I sat in the waiting room straining my eyes looking for my brother, but I couldn't find him. As the minutes ticked away, I became nervous. There were a few hundred people there, but no Mendel. I grew sick at heart, assuming that Mendel had been caught by the Germans, just as I almost was. What would happen if I couldn't find him? Could I go on without him? Should I go back? I was only 17 years old and felt so very alone, but I knew I had to get on that train. There was no going back.

The stories I heard as I waited for the train were horrible and only added to my anxiety. People were talking about the screams of people being taken to be shot. I listened and couldn't say anything. It was so painful to hear. I couldn't find my brother and I felt awful. As I boarded the train I took one last look at the mass of people scurrying to board. Mendel was nowhere to be seen. I felt helpless, but I resigned myself to having lost my brother and knew that I had to go on to save myself.

I had let Mendel know that the train from Odonow to Krakow had a narrow rail, and at Kocmyrzow the train changed to a wider rail. The plan was that we would not get off there, but instead, we would get off at the stop just before Kocmyrzow because I was worried that the Germans would be at the Kocmyrzow station looking for Jews. Then we'd walk to the stop following Kocmyrzow and get back on a train to Krakow. I followed through with that plan. I got off the train and as I walked to the next stop, I kept thinking about my brother. When I reached the station, I sat down on a bench feeling just terrible. I tried to think about seeing Sarah again in the ghetto and being safe – at least for a while -- but all I could think about was Mendel.

Suddenly someone came from behind me and put his hand on my shoulder. It was my brother! He had looked for me at the station in Odonow, but it was so dark and so crowded that he couldn't find me. We were overjoyed to be reunited. For a brief moment there was something to be happy about and from then on we traveled together. We made it to the outskirts of the city, but didn't dare travel on to the main station in Krakow. It wouldn't be safe. There were always too many Germans around.

When we finally arrived at the station on the outskirts of Krakow, we realized we made it! There was a chance for us. When we got off the train, however, a young hooligan suddenly started yelling, "Jew, Jew," and "police, police." I couldn't believe it. We had made it all this way and now we were afraid we were going to get caught. I had to think fast. I would not let it end for both of us since we had gone through so much to get here. I had some single bills in my pocket so I threw them on the ground. When the scoundrel bent down to pick up the money, Mendel and I ran away. We rented a horse and buggy and that was another instance when luck was on our side. It started to rain, so the driver had to cover the buggy to shield us from the weather. I was never so happy to have rain. Now, no one could see us. We told the driver to take us to the restaurant that Moniek had told me about on Miodowa Street.

We arrived at the restaurant, went inside and found the owner. I mentioned Moniek's name and when I started to ask about papers, I got a greeting that I did not expect. She started yelling, "I don't know who you are. Who are you? I have nothing to do with those things. You cannot stay here!" I didn't want to make a scene so I said, "All right, we can't stay here, but can we please have something to eat? A bowl of soup?" She calmed down and I realized she was only putting up a front. She was, in fact, hiding people and helping them with forged Aryan identification papers, but we unfortunately, never got them from her. Everyone in the restaurant seemed tense, upset and guarded. Later I learned that there was a good reason why everyone was nervous, but at that moment, I was puzzled and didn't know where to turn. Moniek wasn't there, and we couldn't get in touch with him. It was impossible to get into the ghetto because we would have been caught and shot if we tried, and there was no one else that we knew in Krakow.

Just as we were wondering what to do next, a Polish man showed us some kindness. He took us to his house and fed us. He didn't turn us away because we were Jewish. He told us it was a very dangerous time to arrive in Krakow. The Gestapo were all over looking for the Jewish communist group that had come into a restaurant and shot some German officers. That was why the woman in the restaurant, and everyone else we encountered, were so nervous.

I wondered if we could possibly make it to the Russian border, but the Polish man said we had no chance and discouraged us. Weleft his place not knowing what to do but knowing clearly what we could not do. He wished us good luck and we thanked him for his compassion. He gave us some hope that there were some decent people left in the world.

It was getting dark and very cold, and we had no place to stay. We saw an empty garbage dumpster in an alley, which luckily was surrounded with a tall fence, so after hearing about the tension in the city we slept in the empty dumpster, hoping no one would find us. The only reason we could get any rest at all was because we were so exhausted.

The following morning we were very hungry. We cleaned up as much as we could and I told Mendel I would go to the bakery nearby to get us something to eat. When I approached the bakery, I was stunned to see that Moniek was there. He had been going into the neighborhood regularly to look for us. After what happened the day before, he was concerned that we had been caught.

Suddenly, I was calm and reassured. For a change things were going our way. I quickly got my brother and followed Moniek as we made our way to the ghetto. Since he was a policeman there, he took us through the gate as prisoners, saying he had caught us in the city. Imagine how happy we were to pass through that gate – happy to be in such a place where life was harsh and cruel. Once we got through the gate, we were able to visit with Sarah while Moniek looked for a place for us to work, since we had no working papers. It would be dangerous for us to remain in the ghetto without papers.

Moniek was able to put us in a group that was being taken to work at the airport in Rakovice that night, so later that day we got into an open truck with the group. I remember it was freezing cold, especially when the truck was moving and the wind whipped through the cargo bed. I had never been so cold before. It seemed to take forever to get to the airport, but eventually we arrived there.

At 15 and 17, my brother and I were so young that we weren't sure how to act. We weren't supposed to be part of the group in the first place. We kept looking at everyone else to see what they were doing, to try to fit in. We found everything so strange. We were watching our every move so we wouldn't call attention to ourselves, but within a short time, we were befriended by someone from Dzialoszyce named Julek, who was pleasant, helpful and showed us the ropes. Later, when I walked into the barrack that I was assigned to in the camp, someone was singing "My Yiddishe Mama." It was too much for me. I broke down, but I took comfort in the fact that at least we were safe for the time being. I knew my father was hiding somewhere, and my sister was safe in the Krakow ghetto. Now we were four.

At the Rakovice airfield we had to build landing strips for jet planes. In 1942, the Germans were already building jet engines, anticipating they would be producing and using jet planes in their war effort. The ground was so cold that we had to use axes and sledgehammers to dig it up. The work was very difficult and the snow was relentless that winter. It was the most severe winter of the war. We had to clear the starting fields so that the planes could take off and land; they were bringing wounded soldiers from the Russian front. The minute we cleaned off one spot, another one would be covered with snow. The work was brutal. We would leave the barracks at 5:30 a.m. and would work until 6 p.m. I used to be so tired that I would sometimes fall asleep standing up, leaning on my shovel.

Every day at noon we got a little soup, but by the time it was given to us, it was cold. At one point we tried to get a little more food. I got some potatoes from a Polish man who worked nearby. When I came back with the potatoes, others had been able to get some too. We cleaned them and put them in a small pot to cook on a little potbelly stove that was in our barrack. We took turns using the stove because it was very small and we couldn't cook all the potatoes at once.

One day I left a few potatoes in the pot that I had placed under my bed. When I came back that night, I quickly put the potatoes on the stove. I had to rush because others were waiting to use the stove. My brother and I started to eat and then looked at each other quizzically. Mendel asked if I had put meat in the pot. I replied, "No," and suddenly felt sick to my stomach. We realized that what we tasted was a cooked mouse that had made the mistake of jumping into the pot. That was the end of our dinner that night. We went outside and threw up. For weeks I could hardly take food in my mouth. It was most unpleasant to say the least. We were both sick, but we survived that too.

Life at the airport was hard, but it was about to become even harder. In January 1943, we were taken to

Plaszow labor camp outside of Krakow. Plaszow was created in 1942 as a labor camp to be run by the SS and Krakow police authorities. The camp was built on two Jewish cemeteries and had four kilometers of electrified barbed wire fencing around its 200 acre property. There were twelve watchtowers with spotlights and guards armed with machine guns. The camp had barracks for German officers and guards, factories, warehouses, as well as separate barracks for men and women. In addition to Jewish prisoners, there were Polish prisoners who were there mostly for holding the wrong political views, but Poles and Jews were separated in the camp and slept in different barracks.

The barracks complex in Plaszow was enormous. Some of the barracks held 500 to 750 people. We slept in three tier bunks. I always chose the top bunk so I wouldn't have anyone above me. The tiers were basically wooden platforms with a little straw, a sheet that I still had from home and a woolen blanket that the Germans supplied. We were also allowed to keep whatever clothes we had on our backs or in our backpacks. We were not issued striped uniforms, but had to wear a yellow patch with a number on it to identify us. In the early stages of Plaszow, the Germans kept us moving from one barrack to another. When we returned from work, we often found our meager belongings on the floor and were told to move to another barrack. That was one of many ways the Nazis tried to dehumanize us.

Plaszow was an awful place. In 1944, it changed from being a labor camp to a concentration camp, but even when it was still considered a labor camp, the

Germans used Plaszow as a dumping ground for the old, the sick and the children swept up in the liquidation of the ghettos. Once they were transported to Plaszow, their final destination was often a mass grave after being stripped and shot. It wasn't that way when the camp first opened, but it became a brutal place starting in 1943.

When Mendel and I arrived at Plaszow in January 1943, Moniek was already there and was a policeman. Since he and my sister, Sarah, had married while in the Krakow ghetto, he took Sarah with him to Plaszow, so the three of us were there. I also met Adolf Klasner when I arrived in Plaszow. He had been the Commander of the Jewish police in Kazimierza Wielka, and also became a policeman in the camp.

Moniek helped us as much as he could. He gave us a decent barrack to live in and was also able to get us work. Sarah worked in the kitchen, and as a result, we were able to get a little more food. Moniek helped get me work as a foreman, overseeing the group of inmates that built the roads. I was very grateful to Moniek because that position gave me some privileges, and because he proved to be there for me when I needed him. I soon realized, however, that the work wasn't the kind of work I liked. Stones and monuments from the Jewish cemeteries were broken up and used to build the roads and some barracks, and I hated desecrating the dead. I also didn't like working outside – especially since it was winter. At night, when we'd walk to the latrine, we would have to walk on the gravestones. It was a very disturbing feeling to know that the graves had been defiled in that way. The Nazis had no regard for human life, nor any respect for the dead. Everything they did was meant to diminish us.

When we first arrived in Plaszow, it was bearable. The commander, a man named Müller, was not so bad. He was a relatively decent man and there were hardly any killings or shootings. We heard stories of other commandants who were far worse. Then, in February 1943, we got a new camp commander – Amon Goeth – and he became our worst nightmare.

Amon Goeth was born in Vienna in 1908. When he was 17 years old, he joined a Nazi youth group. In 1932, he became a member of the Austrian Nazi Party. He was 24 years old then and already showed signs of becoming an infamous monster. The Austrian police chased him into Germany when he was suspected of setting off explosives in the commission of crimes. In Germany, however, he was celebrated as a hero for his terrorist tactics, became a member of the SS, and was eventually given command of Plaszow as a reward for having murdered hundreds of Jews in one of the ghettos.

In his first days at Plaszow, Goeth walked into the construction site of new barracks. There was a dispute between one of the female architects who was Jewish and a male architect who was German. The Jewish architect said that the barracks should be built one way and the German architect wanted to do it another way. Goeth couldn't see a Jew contradict a German, so he told one of the guards to shoot her. The guard asked if he should take her outside and Goeth said, "No, shoot her right here." And that's what he did. She was shot in front of everyone. Then Goeth told the German architect to build the barracks her way. After word spread through the camp about this incident, we knew that there was nothing Goeth wouldn't do to terrorize us and that we were in terrible danger.

Soon after Goeth took over command of Plaszow, my father joined us there. He had left his hiding place and had been living in the Krakow ghetto until its liquidation in March 1943. That was when he was brought to Plaszow. As sad as it was to see my father imprisoned with us, I felt tremendous relief to know that he had not been killed when they liquidated the ghetto. In those horrible times it was a small victory just to be alive and to have part of our family together again. As bad as things were in Plaszow, we took comfort in this alone.

The camp guards were Latvians, Lithuanians, Ukrainians, and Russian prisoners of war who joined the Germans to save their lives. Motivated out of hatred for the Jews, the Ukrainians were often very brutal. When they liquidated the Krakow ghetto and took the Jews to the camp, two young girls, ages seventeen and eighteen, ran away. They were both caught. When they were brought into the camp, they were sentenced to be hanged. The entire camp had to assemble and watch the execution. I was one of those witnesses. We were surrounded by German soldiers with guns. It was horrible to watch, but what happened next was even worse. After the execution Goeth took out his revolver and shot them both in the face. He did that to make it look even more terrifying than just the sight of the two young girls being hung. For Goeth, that was not horrifying enough.

When the shots rang out there was panic and everyone started to run. The assembly area was lit up by spotlights and people scrambled to get as close to the surrounding barracks as possible, to hide in the darkness of their shadows. Finally a voice came over the loud-speaker. It was the voice of Wilek Chilowicz, the commander of the Jewish police in Plaszow. He said he had just spoken to Goeth and was reassured that nothing would happen if we would all just go back to our barracks peacefully. That is exactly what happened; we all quietly filed into our living quarters in an orderly fashion. There was such a sense of resignation. We were beaten down by this man and we knew it. Since I didn't personally witness the female architect being shot, the two girls being executed was my first experience with the unspeakably horrible things that were going on in the camp.

After the liquidation of the Krakow ghetto, in which Goeth actively participated, Goeth said that the children being brought to Plaszow would be given special barracks designated for them. We had an assembly at the roll call place (the *Appellplatz)* and about 300 children were taken from their parents to the middle of the field. Instead of taking them to their barracks, however, the children were put on trucks while lullabies played on the loudspeakers. It was a sadistic measure to torture us. The number of guards was immediately increased. We were all surrounded and were not allowed to move. The parents' screams are impossible to describe as they watched their children being taken away to be killed. Even after all these years, I am still haunted by that scene. The children had no idea they would never see their parents again. Misery and despair fell over the camp after that happened. If our children were our future, the Germans had taken that away from us too. We were a people robbed of our past and our future, forced to endure a horrific present.

Not long afterward, there was an announcement that everyone was to remain in their barracks. Goeth came with his Lithuanian aide, Janetz, to collect all the money and jewelry that people had brought with them from the ghetto. I was lying on my berth with my brother when suddenly Goeth's head popped up beside us and he demanded that we give him our money. I gave him whatever I had -- I had only money, no jewelry. When I went to the outhouse that night, however, I found 150 *zlotys* on the floor behind the latrine. If anyone was found with any money after that day, they would have been shot immediately, but I kept the 150 *zlotys* anyway. Later, it came in handy for food in the black market in the camp.

I could see that life was cheap in Plaszow, and that unless the Germans thought you could be useful, your days were numbered. At one point, when we were assembled for the roll call, I noticed sewing machines that had been taken from Jewish homes and were just rusting away. Goeth was right in front of me when I stepped out of line and said, "Commandant, there is something that I would like to propose. Do you mind if I tell you?" Goeth said, "What is it?" I replied, "I see a lot of sewing machines outside there. I could fix them up and do tailoring with them." He asked if I knew how to do this and I said, "Yes, of course. I was a tailor and worked for my father at my father's shop." Of course I never did, but luckily Goeth believed me and said, "Excellent, I'll give you twenty tailors." He made the announcement at the roll call. Twenty excellent tailors were assigned to the factory, and I became their manager. I supervised them knowing very little about tailoring. In a short time we had a factory ready for production with twenty tailors and twenty shoemakers assigned to work there. Where I got the nerve to step out of line to speak to Goeth, I will never know. I was a young kid. I had an idea and I was too young and stupid to be afraid to suggest it. Typically, when a prisoner was in the line for assembly and stepped out of line even just a little, he could have been killed, but still, I took the chance.

Even though Goeth was a terrifying figure, we felt we would be okay if we could all stay together and be productive. In some ways I was just following my father's example. In 1920 he opened a tailor shop to avoid being sent to the front line in the Polish-Bolshevik War. At that time he knew as much about tailoring as I did, but he did it to save his own life.

Sometimes, at the morning roll call, names were called out and then those people were taken in a transport back to the ghetto, only to return to the camp later that day. That was something the Germans did to try to fool us into believing that being called to board a transport didn't always mean you were going to die. Still, when my brother's name was called, we were sure we were going to lose him. When nothing happened to him we were so relieved, but we were also very nervous for him. We thought they might have taken him because he was so young, so when he came back we changed his name to

Mendel Zelmanowicz – the name of a distant cousin – in order to protect him in the future. He did not have the Fiszler name anymore. We were afraid that the people on that list would be rounded up and taken away again. One could never know what the Germans had in mind.

Every factory in Plaszow had a supervisor. The German that was put in charge of our factory was a very nice older man. He came in one morning and said Goeth was drunk, in a very bad mood and looking for victims, which was so typical of Goeth. He was such an evil, vicious person that sometimes he would kill people for no reason. He would trump up some excuse even though he needed none. The supervisor told me to be careful because Goeth was on his way to the factory. We had twenty shoemakers on one side of the factory and twenty tailors on the other side of the factory. We knew that when Goeth came in we would have to give him a report on the number of people working there. We would have to stand up, say "Achtung," and then make the report to him. If the number was wrong, we could get killed immediately. Moniek Kopec, the manager of the shoemakers, came over to me and said, "I am very nervous. If I get nervous and say something wrong I could get shot. Please make the report for me." I told him not to worry. I would take care of it, but I was as anxious as he was.

Goeth arrived at our factory, with two dogs at his side. As soon as he stepped inside I yelled, "Achtung!" Despite being very nervous, I made the report. I told him how many people were working, how many were sick and about the one I had sent away to get something.

Goeth actually stood there and counted to see if I had made a mistake. I could not believe it. I think he was actually disappointed that I had given him the correct count, but he seemed determined to find fault with me. He then said, "It's now 9 a.m. You started work at 6 a.m. How much did you accomplish today?" After the supervisor's warning, I had prepared work that was done a few weeks before, hoping to satisfy Goeth. But when he saw how much work had been completed, he still was not impressed. He waved his hand and said, "This kind of work I could do myself in three hours; I don't need twenty people to work on it." And as he looked around, I thought we were all about to get shot, but instead he said, "Everyone here will get twenty-five lashes and the foremen (or kapos, as we were called) will get fifty." In a way we were lucky. He'd usually say seventy-five or one hundred lashes. I thought to myself, if these men can take twenty-five lashes, I can take fifty. He left a few guards to watch us and sent for more Ukrainians to carry out the punishment.

Everyone got their twenty-five lashes and the shoemaker kapo, Moniek Kopec, got fifty. I don't know how, but miraculously, I didn't get any. Somehow, I was able to sneak into the group that had already been beaten and I acted as if I was beaten too. The Ukrainians were walking around checking to see if everyone had gotten their lashes, but because we used to fix clothing for the Ukrainians, I had gotten to know some of them. To my surprise, one of the Ukrainians I knew said, "He's got enough. He got more than he was supposed to get." He knew that I didn't get a beating, but because of what he said I was never checked. My own people didn't believe that I got away with it until I proved I was telling the truth by pulling my pants down. I was lucky. Later on I got beatings, but not on that day. I also found out something new about myself that day -- I could act.

Our factory was located on a hilltop, which gave me a perfect view through one of the factory windows to a large area behind the showers. Goeth designated this area as the burial place for the thousands of people, Polish and Jewish, who were brought there to be killed. Whenever I looked out, I could see executions daily. The prisoners were made to undress and lay down in the ditch to be shot. It was horrible. I didn't allow anyone else to look out that window.

Almost no one escaped their fate once Goeth decided to execute them. I say almost no one because there were some people who by some miracle were spared. There was one instance where a man named Grudman and his family were found hiding outside a ghetto after its liquidation. They were brought to Plaszow and made to undress and go into the ditch to be shot. While they were in the ditch, Grudman called out to Goeth. "I have an important thing to tell you, and I will tell you if you will save my life and my family's lives." Goeth asked, "What is it?" Grudman responded, "I have some beautiful horses hidden with a farmer. If you will spare us I will take you to that farmer and you can have the horses." Goeth agreed to the bargain and spared Grudman's and his family's lives.

Goeth had Grudman take care of the horses for him and Grudman was also given some privileges in the camp and received help from Goeth. He was the only one who spoke to Goeth in Yiddish because he didn't know any German. He was the only one who could get away with contradicting Goeth, and it was all because he took care of the horses. As a result, Grudman and his family survived the war. They lived in Neuötting, the town in Germany where I lived after the war. If one were to talk about miracles, that was one of the greatest miracles in the camp.

In the tailoring factory, when we were left alone to do our tailoring and mending, things were not so bad. There were some things that we had to do there, however, that made us sick to our stomachs. One of our tasks was to rip apart clothing that was taken from those who had been shot and killed, to look for money and jewelry. You have to understand that when people were uprooted from their homes and told to get on a transport, they didn't know what awaited them, so they sewed money and jewelry into their clothing. Some of them probably hoped to bargain for their lives with those treasures. Maybe they thought they could use the money and jewelry to buy forged papers and escape across the border. During the occupation, we were accustomed to bribing those in charge for better treatment and to save our lives. Some people hid jewelry that were heirlooms or had sentimental value. We found jewelry in the linings of garments and belts of pants -- in the most unusual places. So it was our grim task to tear apart the garments and to turn over all the valuables and money to Goeth. The clothing was often soaked with dry blood. As strange as it sounds, we all hoped that we would recognize clothing from family or friends so we would learn of their fate. Not knowing the fate of our loved ones was sometimes unbearable. Still, it was sickening to think that the ripping of every stitch, so carefully sewn by someone desperate to stay alive, shred the last trace of their existence on this earth.

As horrible as that was, it got worse. One day while I was still foreman I came into my barracks and discovered that some of the factory workers had taken some of the jewelry, money and diamonds that had been sewn into the clothing. They were trying to find out if the jewelry was real and could be of use to them. I could not believe it. I asked, "What are you people doing? You are endangering every one of us. Do you want to get us all killed?" But my warning was too late.

The Jewish police found out about this incident and told the German supervisor of our factory. They knew that he was a nice man and that he wouldn't tell Goeth. Those workers, however, were taken to the Jewish police station and spent the night in jail. I was brought in the next day and asked by a policeman named, Finkelstein, if I knew anything about the stolen jewelry and money. I said I didn't know anything, but he didn't believe me. When Finkelstein questioned me again, he hit me and I flew across the room, which must have been about 20 feet long. Then he hit me again and demanded that I reveal where the jewelry and money were hidden. I told him I knew nothing about hidden jewelry and money and said, "Look, you can hit me from now until next year. I don't know anything." At that point, Chilowicz, the Jewish commandant of the police, came in and told Finkelstein to stop hitting me. We were all released and

Chilowicz warned us to be more careful or we could all lose our lives. It was a miracle that Goeth didn't find out or we would have been executed.

Following the incident at the police station, I decided I didn't want to be head of the factory anymore. I didn't know enough about the work; I just wanted to be a worker. I went to my brother-in-law and said, "Please help me. I don't want to be a foreman anymore." I had learned that the person who suffered the most when there was trouble was the foreman, despite the fact that there were advantages to the position, such as being given a watch and a double portion of soup. As time went on, however, I realized those extras were not worth it. That's when an older man was selected to be factory manager.

After a while, they had Jewish supervisors take over for the German supervisors in the factory, and that's when a curious incident happened that shaped my future in the concentration camp. Our supervisor was now someone who had been quite active in the Jewish community in the Krakow ghetto. He paid us a visit to introduce himself. The fellow who replaced me as foreman in the factory, then made an uncalled for remark. He commented, "Until now we haven't done too badly, but now since a Jewish supervisor has taken over we are in for trouble." Nobody found his comment amusing. The new supervisor was not pleased at all and told us that we had to change the foreman because this one wasn't smart enough to hold the position. The workers then held an election in the supervisor's office and elected me to run the factory. I couldn't believe that they voted for me to become foreman again, so just as before, I went to

Moniek, my brother-in-law, and pleaded with him. "Please help me. I don't want to be a foreman." He replied, "I can't help you. They voted for you and want you. There is nothing I can do. Just stick it out." I had no choice. I wasn't happy about it then, but now I realize that being a foreman had its advantages in the camp. I was able to get to know some of the German guards; I was able to get more food; I was in a better position to help my father, brother and sister....all things that I wouldn't have been able to do if I was just a worker. Being a foreman helped me survive.

Around this time, we were given new, larger barracks near the quarters of the German guards. We had a separate room for the shoemakers and tailors and another for five barbers. Goeth lived in a villa nearby, which was also close to the quarry (*Steinbruch*). Many who were punished, for any reason, were sent to work in the quarry. Very few survived because the work was brutal. They were constantly beaten and were given very little food. I remember women were harnessed to stone laden carriages that they had to drag away. They wore wooden clogs on their feet, which made it slippery and impossible to navigate the muddy unpaved road, and worked hours and hours. It was extremely harsh punishment for minor occurrences such as being lax at work or having a little more bread than one should have, or trying to steal a potato or something else to eat.

Once, we were all called to the *Appellplatz* after work. We noticed that there were many tables lined up and the number of guards had been increased. After we were all assembled, Goeth selected more than 200 women and made them strip from the waist down. They then had to lie down with their heads on the tables and they were each given 25 to 50 lashes, supposedly for underperforming. Each woman had to count the number of lashes she received. If she miscounted, the whipping would begin again. This was Goeth being entertained by brutality.

In the factory my father, brother and I were together among the 20 other tailors working there. My brother Mendel surprised me by being very capable and learning the tailoring trade quickly while he was in the camp. He knew more than I did even though he was two years younger. While we were in the factory, Moniek arranged for my sister to get a new work assignment, rather than work in the kitchen. Since every block was assigned a leader and an assistant, Moniek made sure Sarah was named assistant to one of the female block leaders. She was not pleased with this, however, even though it gave her a greater chance to survive. Sarah was horrified by what she was forced to witness. People behaved in immoral ways that they never would have done in normal times. Promiscuity was rampant, but it was not unexpected. People were living like animals and took pleasure where they could find it. For my sister, however, it was overwhelming and she was haunted by suspicions – rightly or wrongly – that Moniek was having an affair with another woman.

In the early days of 1943, we were allowed to visit the women's quarters from 6 p.m. to 9 p.m. before we had to return to our barracks to sleep. However, those few hours of companionship and of being able to spend time with her family were not enough to lift my sister's spirits. Sarah was very sensitive and could not cope with life in the camp. She saw people tortured by Goeth, which was unbearable for her. Goeth would gather the block leaders and look for excuses to punish and torture them. He was a sadist who terrified Sarah. Once, unbeknownst to her, I was walking behind her while she was speaking to Wilek Chilowicz, the Jewish police commander who tried to help and protect her. I heard her say that she couldn't take it anymore. She had to witness Goeth torturing and beating the leaders and she lived in fear that she would be singled out for that as well. Chilowicz tried to reassure her that he would see to it that she wouldn't be harmed, but who could keep such a promise under these circumstances? She hated that her husband was a policeman. He was no longer the sweet man she had met in the lobby of that cockroach-infested hotel, the man she had spent the night talking to, and the man who had become a member of our family. He was hardened, bitter and disliked. Sarah felt isolated and full of despair. To make matters worse, she never got over losing our mother. For Sarah, life was too hard. She couldn't go on living for one more day in this hell on earth. In 1944, she was able to get some pills and committed suicide.

I was called when she was taken to the barrack that had been converted to a hospital run by Jewish doctors from Krakow. She was unconscious and suffered for two days. Before she passed away she tried to speak to me but couldn't. Her voice was gone. She was probably going to apologize for what she did, but she didn't have to do that for me. I tried to comfort her as best as I could, but I felt so helpless. As she struggled in those last days, my mind drifted back to the happier times we had before this evil madness began. I remembered her laugh, her smile, the way she first talked about Moniek after they met, and the way my mother and Sarah planned and dreamed about the wedding she would have. Sarah seemed to have such a bright future ahead, with a loving husband and the promise of beautiful things to come. Even now, she still looked so lovely despite all that she had been through. Chilowicz came to see her after she died and said, "Sarah, you were so beautiful before you died and you are still just as beautiful now." Chilowicz received permission from the commandant to permit me to give Sarah a normal burial rather than having her thrown into a mass grave. My father, brother and I carried Sarah to a single grave and buried her. I cannot imagine the pain that my father felt at that time. How much pain can a person endure?

I wrote Sarah's name on a piece of paper and put it in a bottle which I buried with her. I was hoping that if I, or anyone from my family, survived the war we could go to the site of the camp and locate the spot where she was buried. When I returned to Plaszow many years later, there was nothing left of the camp. There were just two monuments and many homes built where the barracks had stood and where all the torturing and killing had taken place. It was as if nothing had happened there. It was surreal. How sad that on that site where such tragedies happened, children were playing and people were living in homes with beautiful gardens. There was no way for me to find the place where Sarah was buried. Like so many others, her body would never be found.

My brother-in-law hardened even more after Sarah committed suicide. Perhaps he felt responsible in some way for what she did. I don't know and I never will know. He never said it, but there was no question that he had become harsh and cold. It wasn't only losing my sister that embittered him, but also losing his mother and then my mother, to whom he was also very close. He became resentful and jealous of others.

After Sarah's death, I cried night and day. It wasn't just about what I had lost; it was about going through all the emotions of this horrible experience. It seemed like such a terrible waste to lose Sarah that way. It made me angry – not with her – but with what this war was doing to all of us. I refused to let the war defeat me, however. I woke up each morning thinking we were one day closer to liberation. For me, living was still better than not living. I had something to hold onto. My father and my brother were still alive and I was still hoping that maybe I could help them survive. Perhaps there was still a slim chance for us.

We began to hear horrible stories from the world outside of the camp of people being shot and gassed to death. I had no doubt people were being murdered because I saw it with my own eyes, but I never believed the extent of what actually was going on. If you're alive, you always have hope. I was strong and knew that eventually there would be an end to the war. But when would that happen? How long would it take? Would we survive? Some of us ran out of patience and began to take risks to make sure we would survive the war. Chilowicz, who had shown my sister such kindness, was one of those people. One day I saw him sitting on the steps in front of our factory. He told me he was waiting for a Russian guard to meet him there. Many of the Russian prisoners of war sided with the Germans and became guards – most likely to save their own lives. I had a premonition and told Chilowicz that if he was making a deal with this Russian, it was a mistake. I said, "I don't trust him. He's always with the Germans. There's something wrong with him." Dismissing what I told him, he replied, "I know him well, and in a few days you'll hear that I'm famous." I walked into the factory and saw Chilowicz outside pacing very nervously. I realized then I could not reason with him. He was determined to go through with his plan.

On Sunday morning we heard that Goeth had hatched a plot against Chilowicz. He set up the Russian guard to sell a revolver to Chilowicz and made arrangements for Chilowicz, his brother-in-law, his sister, his wife, Marisia – who as a female commandant was hated in the camp – and the Jewish policeman named Finklestein (the one who had beaten me earlier), to run away. They all got into a garbage truck, but as they came to the gate to escape from the camp, Goeth was there waiting. They were all shot and killed.

Why did Goeth kill them? Through the years when Chilowicz was commander of the Jewish police in the camp, Goeth took a lot of the food that was designated for us, as well as jewelry and other valuables that had been taken from the Jews, and sold it on the black market in Krakow. He, however, couldn't sell it on the black market himself so he had Chilowicz do his dirty work.

Because Chilowicz knew too much, Goeth had to eliminate him. After Chilowicz, his family and Finkelstein were killed, they were laid out in front of a barrack. Goeth made all the prisoners walk past them to illustrate what would happen to anyone who tried to run away. Chilowicz's death was a devastating blow to us because we all felt that if anyone had a chance to survive, it was Chilowicz. However, that didn't mean we weren't tempted to take a chance to escape anyway.

Our factory was not far from the gate. At one point the gate was open and not guarded. I watched and then called someone else to watch because I knew that if anyone ran away, a hundred or more people would be shot as a reprisal. I could have run away many times, but I knew that if I ran away others would die. The first to be punished would be my father and my brother, and I couldn't carry that on my conscience.

Life in Plaszow was very harsh. At its largest, there were about 25,000 inmates. There was little food and people were starving. The morning rations consisted of a little dark water that passed as coffee, with a piece of bread and some margarine, and occasionally some jam. At noon we got some thin soup, and in the evening we got the same watery soup with a piece of bread. No one could survive on these very limited rations for long, especially since the work was so strenuous. What made it even worse was living with the constant fear that I could lose my life at any time.

Hunger prevailed, but I was able to get a little more food for my people by making uniforms for the Germans and the guards. That was a great help. I knew the Russian cook and was able to go to the Russian and Ukrainian guards' kitchen after their meals to get their leftovers. He kept them for me and I would bring back a pail of soup or whatever else was available and divide it equally among the tailors, shoemakers and barbers in our barrack. Somehow I was lucky. I got to know the people who could help me and they took a liking to me. I took chances and was able to get what others could not.

It was very dangerous to bring in food from the outside. I remember that once, a group of forty inmates were taken to work outside of the camp at Madritsch, a sewing company. They were able to get a little more food, on the black market including loaves of French bread. Goeth, however, was waiting at the gate when they returned. They were searched and because they had bread and other food, all forty were taken to the hill – Chujowa Gorka – and shot. All forty of them were murdered for a mere few loaves of bread. After that incident, everyone was afraid to bring black market food into the camp even though they were starving.

I tried to find other ways to get food for my workers and me. Because I was a foreman, I had access to a German warehouse where I found some wool fabric that I took back to the factory. We worked together to cut the fabric to make pants, especially for the Russian guards who were helpful and supportive to us in many ways. They were Russian POWs who had been brought to Plaszow to work as guards. I also made a pair of pants for a German named Sorenson who later assumed a senior position in Plaszow. He ended up having a major impact on my survival.

Once after a very productive day at work, a few weeks after the incident with the 40 people from Madritsch, all 45 of us lined up -- 20 tailors, 20 shoemakers and 5 barbers -- ready to be marched off to our living quarters. Schupke, our German supervisor, who was kind to us, was there to check and count us before we departed to our barracks. There were rumors that Schupke was responsible for the murder of some Jews in another camp, but we never knew for sure if it was true. Who knew if he had a change of heart and tried to make up for his past deeds by treating us well? All I can say is that on this particular day we owed our lives to him. Goeth walked down from his villa and came over to us. We were carrying our canteens, which were supposed to be empty but were filled with all kinds of food from the black market that we had bought from the guards. We were bringing the food back for ourselves and for our families and friends. You can imagine our fear. All Goeth had to do was call out for any one of us to be searched and I would not be here. Goeth approached and Schupke saluted him, stating, "The group is assembled and ready to be marched off to their living quarters. I have checked everything and everything is in order." Luckily, I don't think that Goeth wanted to contradict him, so he said, "Now you can all go." Goeth then walked away.

That was my closest brush with death to date. It was nothing less than a miracle that we survived. I can't believe that all 45 of us kept our faces emotionless, not showing any fear. All I thought of was the incident with the people who had returned from Madritsch. I really believe that God was watching over us. There is no other explanation for how lucky we were.

On another occasion, I had a terrible incident with a Russian officer who was a guard. He came to pick up work, which was not ready. There was so much work we couldn't keep up with it, and as a result, I got a beating. I decided again that being the foreman was too dangerous for me and I gave it up. I made too many promises to get extra food for us, and it was beginning to take its toll on me. Someone else took over and did a good job because he was too afraid to bend or break the rules. However, he was sent away in a transport and once more I had to take over as foreman.

When there were 20 tailors working in the factory, guards who brought in work weren't allowed to come inside. They had to hand the clothing through a tiny window unless they had to try it on. One day I looked through the window and my heart stopped beating. Goeth was standing there, watching us work. Luckily everyone was working at their machines. I just had to walk around making myself look busy too. I walked over to a man by the name of Mr. Wind and said, "Mr. Wind, I don't think this is the way you should do it. Change it. Let's do it this way." Wind looked at me and I was afraid he would say, "Who the hell are you to tell me how to do this work?" I knew nothing and he was so talented, so I didn't give him a chance to say it. I turned to Goeth and I yelled, "Achtung" and everybody got up. He looked at us and said, "Go back to work," and walked away. We were just fortunate that everyone was hard at work when he came by. Luck was with us again.

In the spring of 1944, there were frequent transports coming from and going to Plaszow. There were transports with Jews from Hungary that stopped on the way to Auschwitz, which was about 35 miles away. I recall that a transport of about 2,000 women was brought to Plaszow. Their heads were shaved and they were wearing striped uniforms. Despite that, some of them were so beautiful. They didn't know that in a day or two their destination was Auschwitz and that they would likely be sent to the gas chambers there. Indeed, I've read that following a selection, on one day alone - May 14, 1944 - about 1,400 Jews were sent from Plaszow to Auschwitz and were immediately sent to the gas chambers.

The Russian army started its advance in the summer of 1944. The Germans began their preparations to close Plaszow and every week another transport of a few thousand was sent somewhere, most of the time to other camps in the West, away from the eastern front. The Germans planned to take us closer to the German border, away from the advancing Russians, but suddenly the Russians stopped their advance to regroup about sixty miles from our camp. They remained there for six months without moving. Every day we looked through the gates and the fences and saw German troops moving back and forth heading to and from the front. We were on edge, hoping something would happen soon. Every day that went by made us even more anxious. Did the Russians not know what was happening here? People were dying and the Russian front was so close to us, so frustratingly close, and yet so far.

Goeth was arrested by the Germans in September 1944, for selling prisoners' food on the black market as well as keeping some of the money and jewelry stolen from the Jews, for himself. While it was acceptable to steal from Jews, it was not acceptable that he had stolen from the German Reich.

Soon after Goeth left we received a package that included salami and other food from the Red Cross. It was the first time that we had been treated decently. It was a sign - a brief respite - of better days for us. After Goeth was arrested, Sorenson, took over the day-to-day administration of the camp. We had done a lot of work for him and I had a decent history with him. As mentioned earlier, he was one of the Germans I had made pants for from the wool in the warehouse. I could have gotten in trouble for taking the wool, but I was very fortunate because one day he commented, "You know I'm missing some wool material from the warehouse. Do you know anything about it?" He was wearing the pants I had made from it, so I asked, "Did you ever look at your pants?" He figured it out and left without another word. I was very lucky. Maybe it was more than just luck. Maybe someone from above was watching over me.

By the end of 1944, there were only about 400 of us left in Plaszow. My brother was taken on a transport during that time. Once again, tragedy struck. I was heartbroken. I did everything possible to try to rescue him from the transport. I said, "I am here with my father and my brother. Please don't break up our family. If you can release my brother, I will go on the transport in his place." I fought so hard to change places with him because I thought that he might have a greater chance of survival if he stayed in Plaszow. I knew that I was stronger and had a better chance to live if I were on the transport. I was powerless to do anything but plead for his life. There were just a few Jewish police left. Moniek, my brother-in-law, wasn't there anymore; he too had been taken away on a transport. All the connections that I had made were gone. It just wasn't meant to be. What I was told was that if my brother had our family name, either he would not have gone or we all would have been taken. Who knows?

Had we made a terrible mistake by changing his name, or did changing his name spare my father and me? With what we went through in those last few months, who knows what would have happened? There were so many ifs. I just know that if Mendel was shot I would have been shot too, because I would have joined him. There is no doubt in my mind. At the time I just hoped that wherever they took him, he might survive.

I watched my brother walk to the train, and just like my mother before, he was the only one who was crying. I will never forget the expression on his face. He looked like a little boy in some ways – the little boy who cried and looked so sad and afraid when he scraped his knee or had a bad dream and ran to our mother for comfort. There was no such comfort for him – or for me – now.

When Mendel was taken away, many thoughts went through my mind. Perhaps the transport would return the way it did the last time. Of course, I knew it wouldn't. Maybe Mendel would be sent to another forced labor camp or assignment. He was young and strong, and could still be useful to the Germans. Although I hoped with all my heart that I was wrong, deep down I knew I would never see him again. Now we were two.

My father and I remained in Plaszow with about four hundred others. The factory was reduced to two men, but we were expected to operate in the same fashion that we did when there had been twenty tailors.

Despite that, life was a little easier in the camp from November 1944 to January 1945. Since there were so few of us remaining, we were able to salvage the best bedding and set up living quarters for ourselves in an empty guard barrack. For a few precious weeks, we had more food than we had had before. There were no shootings during this time either. Life in the camp became more civilized. Every Sunday afternoon there were concerts performed by musicians who previously had been commanded to play exclusively for Goeth. One night a week we even had dances.

We knew Plaszow would be liquidated eventually, and those few weeks between November and January turned out to be the calm before the storm. One January night at 11 p.m. there was a bombing by Russian planes. We knew something was happening. The Russian offensive had started - the one that had been stalled for six months. One of those Russian bombs injured a SS man working in the camp. When he came to the factory showing us a wound on his neck, we were delighted but had to show no emotion. After all we had seen and experienced, a wounded German was not someone we could feel sympathy for. We were anxious about what would happen next - we didn't care what had happened to him. The following evening they assembled the final 400 of us and told us that the camp was closing. We had thought we were going to be taken to Częstochowa, Poland, where a camp was being prepared to take us, so when we learned we were not going to Częstochowa, we feared we would be marching off to our death. Our terrible journey was not over. The front was so close to us, but freedom was still very far away. We came to realize that so much more awaited us.

(top) *A candlestick from my childhood home – the only thing I have left from my family. Years after the war I received it from our former landlady. She saved it, hoping that someday a family member would return.* (bottom) *My cousin, Mania Morawiecka, who was killed by the Nazis before she received her papers to emigrate to the United States.*

(top) *My granddaughter, Melissa, and I in front of my childhood home in Kazimierza Wielka.* (center) *At the end of the road on the left is another view of my childhood home - the apartment building in which my family and I lived until the liquidation of our Jewish community.* (bottom) *Years after the war I returned to visit the orchard where my cousin, Abram Fiszler, and I spent our summers.*

Rhoda and I are grateful for our daughter, Laura, son-in-law, Ronen Wilk, and our dear grandchildren, Ariel and Daniel.

Our son, David, has given us so much joy over the years, as have our two wonderful grandchildren, Brian and Melissa. We are so blessed!

(top) *Rhoda - the love of my life - and I on our wedding day.* (bottom) *After the war, my father stayed in Germany where he settled down with a German woman sympathetic to the plight of the Jews. Despite his living in Germany, we were still able to get together regularly and he was blessed to live long enough to get to know his grandchildren.*

(top) *The place where my mother, my two brothers and my sister hid when the Jewish community in Kazimierza Wielka was liquidated. It's where I said goodbye to them for the last time.* (center) *The Slonowice woods memorial erected to honor the Jews killed there during the liquidation of Kazimierza Wielka.* (bottom) *A local man telling my childhood friend, Sam Rakowski, and me about the Jews being murdered in the Slonwice woods; a place where I spent many happy hours as a child prior to the war.*

(top) *My school in Kazimierza Wielka. In 1942, this is where the Jews who came out of hiding were kept until they were later taken to the Slonowice woods and killed there. (bottom) The building where we held meetings for our Hashomer Haleumi club. This Zionist youth organization inspired its members to be tough and resilient.*

After the war, my close friends became my family. (top – left to right) *Me and Max Greenberg after a DP camp soccer game.* (bottom- left to right) *Ben Krotowski, his wife Genia (Jean), Ida and Leon Fruchtman.*

(top) *One of my fondest memories of my youth is playing soccer. This team is from my DP camp. I am the one sitting in the first row.* (bottom) *On a trip back to Poland I visited the same alley where my brother and I hid in an empty dumpster on our first night in Krakow…not unlike the one*

(top - left) *My Aunt Bella, my mother's sister, who sponsored my immigration to the United States, standing outside her home in Brooklyn. She walked with a crutch which is visible in this picture.* (top-right) *Here I am in America, standing in front of my Aunt Bella's home.* (bottom) *My dad remained in Germany, but did have a chance to visit Israel. Here he is praying at the Wailing Wall in Jerusalem*

(top) *Had it not been for Roman Sikorski's decision to risk his life by hiding my sister and me during the liquidation of our Jewish community, I would not have lived to write this book. I was thrilled to meet his daughter, Musia, on a trip to Poland years after the end of the war.* (bottom) *Rhoda and I with the three boys from Rockville Centre, N.Y. (Zach, Michael and Luke) and their families in Poland. I taught them about my Holocaust experiences as part of their Bar Mitzvah project, and traveled with them to Warsaw, Krakow, Plaszow, Auschwitz and my hometown of Kazimierza Wielka.*

I started the war as a teenage boy. By the time the war ended and I was liberated, I was a 20-year-old man. The time I spent in Germany after the war (1945-1949) was a period of adjustment and a time for reflection. I couldn't make up for the childhood I lost, but the longer I was in the DP camp, the more eager I became to start a new life.

In January 1945 we were ordered to leave Plaszow labor camp. After the war a monument was built to honor those who died there.

Chapter Four
Then We Were Two

Plaszow, our personal hell on earth, was finally closed, but now a new hell awaited us. We were not told where we were going, only that we were leaving permanently and ordered to start marching. First, we marched through the city of Krakow. I could have easily run away, but it was difficult to do because my father was with me. I knew that if I ran away and left him behind, he would be shot immediately. Of course, if I ran I had no idea where I would go or how long it would take for the war to end. There were so many times when we thought it would be only a number of days or weeks before we'd be liberated…and then months went by and nothing happened.

The night we started our march to the unknown, there was a terrible ice storm. We did not know where we were heading, but later learned that we were going to Auschwitz, about 35 miles away. The ground was so frozen, slippery and treacherous that we had to hold on to each other for support. I recall an incident with a friend, Irka Salomonowicz, who said to me after we had walked several miles, "Isn't this terrible? When we left Plaszow we looked half human but were reasonably healthy, and now we look disabled."

When we began the march to Auschwitz, every one of us was given some bread. We marched through Sunday night and the whole day Monday. Close to midnight on the 14th of January 1945, we arrived at Auschwitz – where we were greeted by the sign, "Arbeit Macht Frei" (work makes one free). The terrible stench of burned human flesh and the sight of piles of skeletons, however, told us that that was a lie. Before we had left Plaszow, the Germans ordered us all to dig up the mass graves and to burn the human remains so that there would be no trace of their crimes. I couldn't believe how awful the burning flesh smelled. When I arrived at Auschwitz that same horrible stench greeted me, and I knew immediately what it was. I realized that all the rumors that I had heard about this place were true. Auschwitz was a death camp. The Germans were doing everything to erase any signs of their crimes and to eliminate as many of their witnesses as possible. We wondered what would become of us now? We knew the Germans did not want any witnesses to their atrocities to survive so our outlook was very bleak.

After midnight we were taken to the showers. We had heard rumors about the gassings so we turned our heads toward the showerheads in fear, not knowing if water or poison gas would pour over us. To our relief water came raining down. We took our showers and were given striped prisoners' uniforms for the first time. Our personal clothing which we had been able to wear up until this time was taken away. Then we went to our assigned barracks. The kapos (supervisors) of each of these barracks were murderers who had been released from German prisons specifically to work as kapos. They were incredibly cruel. They hit and screamed at us -- especially because we were newcomers to the camp. Their barking dogs added to the terror. Their intent was to obtain complete obedience from us through fear. We never knew what was going to happen next.

Luckily our stay at Auschwitz only lasted four days. On January 18th, we were told to gather on the *Appellplatz*. That day 60,000 inmates left Auschwitz on the death march, in groups of 3,000 each. We were each given a loaf of bread and a woolen blanket. It was a cold, beautiful sunny day, and the ground was covered with snow. We could sense the urgency of the Germans' actions and their tension, because the Russian Army was rapidly advancing. We marched all night through an incredibly windy blizzard, traveling south 40-45 miles toward Gleiwitz, Poland – a sub-camp of Auschwitz – near the border of Czechoslovakia. Our meager clothing was no match for the wintry conditions. Even the German guards were freezing during the terrible blizzard, despite the fact that they had heavy coats, hats and gloves. You can imagine how horrific it was for us. I remember approaching the Polish-Czech border and asking myself if the whole world had forgotten about us. Did anyone care about us Jews who were being persecuted beyond human comprehension?

The following day we arrived in Gleiwitz. They took away our leather shoes and gave us wooden shoes. We were housed in one of the barracks where we remained for only one day. Eight of us were crammed into a little room, the size of a small closet. We did not sleep that night because the Russians were bombing the town. I remember looking out the door and seeing the light from the Russian incendiaries lighting up the town like daylight. Because of that bombing there was a sense of heightened urgency that we had not experienced before. We didn't know how to feel about the bombing – we were either on the verge of destruction or liberation. The tension in the air was thick. We had no idea what would happen next.

The following evening we were herded into open freight train cars. At that time we numbered about 3,000, with 100 of us in each open car. It was snowing and brutally cold again. That was an exceptionally brutal winter. We used our blankets to cover our thin striped uniforms, which gave us minimal coverage and warmth. I was put in one of the first train cars and my father was separated from me for the first time since his arrival in Plaszow. I told my friend Leon Fruchtman that after daybreak, I was going to get out of our freight car to search for my father. He told me I shouldn't do it because I would be shot. No one was ever allowed to leave the train for any reason whatsoever, but I wouldn't listen to Leon. I was determined to find my father.

I couldn't look for my father at night because I definitely would be shot, so I waited until morning to get out of the train car. Leon was sure I wouldn't be able to do it, but I was very worried about my father so I took a tremendous risk to find him.

There were about thirty freight cars and I had to find a way to walk by each one without being shot. Fortunately, the train stopped frequently in various stations to refill the locomotive with water, so at one of the stations, I got out. As I passed by each car I yelled 'father' in Polish (tatuś) and waited for a response. There was one train car that held Jewish scientists who were working for the German war industry, and who were supervised by a German SS officer named, Miller. I knew Miller because he had supervised the scientists in Plaszow and we had done work for him in our factory. Luckily the scientists were in a car near the end of the train, so when the guards stopped me and asked me where I was going, I told them that Miller had sent for me. That was how I was able to go from car to car searching for my father.

Eventually, I found the car where my father was, and I climbed into it. One of the prisoners with us, Meyer

Bochenek, never forgot what I called out to find my father so we could be reunited again. Meyer survived the war and whenever he saw me after that day, he called me "tatuś." He often referred to this incident as one of his most memorable. I risked my life to find my father but it was worth it. He was the only member of my family that I had left and I didn't feel I could go on without him. Fortunately, we were never separated again.

As we traveled in the open train cars, snow fell on us day and night without stop. Our blankets and light clothing were inadequate against the wind and snow that ripped through the car. One advantage of being packed so tightly in the open car, however, was that our body heat warmed us to a certain degree. People, though, were running out of bread and starving. My father, ever resourceful, somehow kept a little sugar with him in the event we would need it. How he was able to keep that sugar with him is still a mystery to me, but it allowed us to mix a few grains of sugar with snow every day to give us a little more strength than we could get from just the piece of bread.

When we traveled through Czechoslovakia we were pleased that some people responded to our plight by throwing us food. Once, when we were going through Prague, some Czechs threw some bread into the train cars from a bridge. I was lucky to grab a piece and that kept me going a little longer. We had to use enormous restraint to limit ourselves to a meager piece of bread daily since we did not know when we would get more food or for how long we would be on the train. Unfortunately others did not share my luck; there were many deaths from starvation and the severe cold. When any of the prisoners died we threw the body off the train to let the rest of the world know what was happening to us. In this small way, we defied the Germans. We were supposed to keep the bodies with us in the train car so that the Germans would have our exact head count once we arrived at our destination. But, at the same time, with each death, we gained a little more room in the open car, enabling some of us to sit in shifts. One night I tried to sit down and rest, but some of the other prisoners sat on top of me. They wanted to get my bread and thought that I was dead. I had a needle in my lapel, which I used as a weapon. I started yelling, "I'm not dead yet, I'm not dead." It was the only way to keep them off of me.

We were in those open cars two and one-half to three weeks, going from one place to another as the Germans tried to find a place to take us. As a result, we lost track of time. As horrific as those open cars were, later we learned that the closed train cars were even worse.

On the way to Austria the train took us past Dresden where there was a terrible firebombing in progress. Our train was detoured into the woods where we stopped. We remained there for the whole night, anxious and fearful because we knew that whenever they took us into the woods there was a chance that we would be killed. The incendiaries were lighting up the sky like fireworks. We braced ourselves for the possibility that we would be made to strip and climb into a ditch to be slaughtered, or that we'd be targets for the bombs. We remained in the train all night, not knowing what was happening, nor what would happen next. We thought that this might be the end because we realized that this bombing was out of the ordinary.

Much to our surprise, the next morning our trip resumed to an unknown destination. We traveled for a day or two until we arrived at Mauthausen, a concentration camp in Austria. They would not accept us because ironically, the camp was full. We feared that if there was no room for us, they'd have no reason to keep us alive. What we didn't realize was that we were an asset to the Germans who were in charge of us. We were lucky once again – lucky that those Germans were so concerned about being sent to the Russian front that they did everything possible to keep us alive. By that time they realized their war was a lost cause and keeping us alive enabled them to avoid being sent to the front lines.

When we were turned away from Mauthausen we stopped in Dresden again to fill the locomotives with water. Dresden was a ghost town. There was not a person to be seen. That was the result of the allied firebombing that had taken place the night we stayed in the woods. The commander of the transport went into each car, randomly selected ten prisoners, and shot them right there, in the station. Whether he did that as a reprisal for Dresden's firebombing or because we didn't have enough bodies to show when we arrived at our destination, I'll never know. All I know is that when he came into any car he could have selected anyone – my father, me or anyone else. My father and I were fortunate that we were not selected, but this random selection only intensified our fears.

As we resumed our train journey we saw signs that indicated that we were 90 kilometers from Berlin. We also traveled through the city of Leipzig where amazingly we saw trolleys, buses and people going about their business, as though life was normal. When we traveled through the Sudeten Mountains we saw colorful villas, as well as beautiful snow covered mountains. We couldn't get over those glorious views. We were so hungry and desperate, but at the same time we could still appreciate the beauty of the countryside. Our hearts were bleeding wondering why some people lived beautiful, normal lives, while just because we were Jewish we had to suffer like this. Why did they do this to us?

By the time we arrived in Oranienburg, Germany – at another concentration camp outside of Berlin – we had suffered tremendous human losses since leaving Auschwitz more than three weeks earlier. Our train was unloaded. That was the first time that we had gotten off the train. Much to our surprise, the German supervisor unloading our train was Sorenson, the German that I had made pants for in Plaszow! Several months earlier he had been transferred from Plaszow to an unknown destination. It was a miracle that with the millions of men in the German army, he was the one who met us. The group from Plaszow was kept together and we hoped that Sorenson would remain with us. We were taken to a camp at the Firma Heinkel air force base near Berlin where Heinkel planes were manufactured. After all those weeks of sleeping in trains, we now slept in the airport hangar on a cement floor covered with a bit of straw. We still had our woolen blankets for additional warmth. We were there for one week. During that time sirens were continuously going off warning that bombers were coming, but we were not afraid. From our recent train travel experiences, we knew that Germany was not the safe haven that Hitler had promised its citizens. He had promised them that no enemy plane would ever bomb a German city.

After a week in Oranienburg, more than 300 of us survivors were taken in locked freight train cars to Flossenbürg, another dreadful concentration camp in Germany. That was my first experience of traveling in locked freight cars, with the only light being that which came in through the cracks in the car walls. There was one sanitary pail for the 100 passengers in each car. For me, that claustrophobic experience was shattering…but at least I was with my father. I thought of my brother who had to travel in a train car like this all alone. We were constantly haunted by not knowing where we were being taken. When we arrived at Flossenbürg, we were taken through the gates to the barracks, and just as in Auschwitz, we passed mountains of skeletons and the stench of burned bodies was overwhelming. The same sign that we had seen at Auschwitz, "Arbeit Mach Frei," also greeted us. It was very obvious to me that the Flossenbürg prisoners we saw were dying of hunger and other brutal conditions. Until today I do not know if Flossenbürg had a gas chamber, but there was no doubt that the Germans murdered people there in droves.

In Flossenbürg, we were put into a barrack, told to take off our clothing, and checked for cleanliness and lice. Unfortunately, but not unexpectedly, they found a louse on my body. The last time I had bathed was in

Auschwitz, more than a month ago, so that was not unexpected. It was February and I had to lie in a freezing cold, tin-lined sink that ran the length of the room, with ice cold water running over me for almost a half hour. To me it seemed endless. That was to punish me as well as to clean me. I don't know how I survived that ordeal, but I guess that my determination to survive and the extra food I had gotten when I was at Plaszow, built up my strength enabling me to survive. I think others likely would have died under the same circumstances.

After a week in Flossenbürg we were on the road again. We traveled by train to Plattling, Germany, again in closed freight cars. As we got off the train, Sorenson met us. I had not seen him since our meeting at the train station in Oranienburg, about two weeks earlier. I said a prayer to God for watching over me, again.

We were kept in a school for one week as they prepared a camp for us. The city was bombed while we were housed in the school. Part of the ceiling collapsed, but luckily we were on the other side of the room and no one was injured. The following day we were taken to clean the streets and some buildings. Although it was hard labor we did not mind since the devastating destruction that we saw let us know that the Germans were also suffering. There were rumors that as a result of the bombing a few thousand people had been trapped and killed in a matter of minutes that day.

The camp in Plattling was next to the airport. Once we got settled, people were taken to forced labor. Although both the quality and quantity of the food we were given improved, because we were now getting more than the average slave laborer, the amount of food was still insufficient and there was severe hunger. People were dying of starvation because some prisoners were so malnourished from their previous experiences that they simply had no chance to survive.

When we got to the camp, Sorenson put my father and me in a large room in the barrack with two beds with straw mattresses, two sewing machines and some sewing supplies. Sorenson informed us that we were to open a sewing factory for the Germans and the kapos who had come with us. Little did he know that in Plaszow I had twenty tailors. Here I had my father – who had some tailoring skills but was now too weak to work – and myself. Fortunately, by this time I had learned more about tailoring from my experience in Plaszow. It was a challenge, however, to keep up with the workload since we were only two people. My prior experience was managing the tailors in Plaszow, but now I was expected to do the work myself. I was at a loss. I didn't know how I would be able to do it, but once again, I had a lucky break.

A Lithuanian Jewish man named Gelczynski approached me and asked, "Could you help me? I'm here with my brother and he will definitely not survive the war if he has to work outdoors. The winter is too harsh for him and he's not strong enough. I need to find some indoor work for him. He's an excellent tailor. Would you take him into your factory?" That was music to my ears. I said I would take him in and see what I could do. The only problem was that it was a small camp and the

Germans only allowed two tailors. I had to come up with a solution to this problem. Since I was not allowed to report that he was working for us, every day during the roll call assembly I hid Gelczynski's brother under my bed. Because he was big, I had to raise the bed over him, and then he'd crawl under. During the roll call, when his name was called, I'd answer for him. I don't know how, but somehow I got away with it. Was it luck on my part or was it because the Germans and kapos knew me and let me get away with it? I will never know. All I know is that we were never caught. That was another miracle…and miraculously, the Gelczynski brothers survived the war. We were in the same displaced persons camp in Germany after the war's end. Later on, they settled in New York, as did I, and we saw each other many times.

Plattling, the site of our new camp, is a town in Bavaria and was Germany's meat slaughtering center. Once, Sorenson took me with him when he went to the slaughterhouse to order some food for the camp. While there Sorenson asked me to carry a large piece of liver back to the camp for him. If he had been caught carrying it, he would have been punished because food was strictly rationed, even for the German military. So, how could I get the liver back to the camp for him? I had no place to hide it. He gave me a newspaper to wrap it in so I put the liver under my belt between my shirt and pants. While we were returning to the camp, however, we crossed an open field during a bombing. I had no choice but to lie down on the grass. What a mess I made. You can imagine how I looked when I walked back into the camp with blood all over me. Everyone thought I had been wounded, but I managed to get Sorenson his liver. Still, rumors circulated throughout the camp that the tailor had been wounded.

When Nuremberg fell to the Americans, about 50 German planes escaped and came to the Plattling Airport. We were having our usual roll call when a few Allied planes flew over our camp and the airport. Most likely they spotted the planes and probably photographed them and us. Our hopes were raised because we thought the world would learn of our plight. The next day, the Allied planes returned and destroyed every single plane on the ground with machine guns and bombs. Since we were so close to the airport we had to hide in a ditch. We ran from one side of the ditch to the other. When the bombing stopped we crawled out of the ditch and there were empty shells in the ditch and all around. Once again, we were lucky that no one was hurt or killed.

We were in Plattling from the end of February until April 27, 1945. We marched out of Plattling that day, but this time it was not a death march. The Germans showed little interest in killing us. They now realized they had to stay one step ahead of the Allies or they would be overrun. We had a high-ranking German officer in our camp who was part of the Organization Todt (OT), who seemed to be a decent human being. The OT group was comprised of engineers who were responsible for building and maintaining military buildings and fortifications, railroad bridges, roadways, and civilian air raid shelters. They were different from the SS. This officer informed our camp leader that he was sending a food truck to accompany us, so that at every stop we could be fed. My father and I personally knew him because we had made some repairs to his uniform on more than one occasion. I had also gone to his quarters, where I did some tailoring for his wife. She too was a decent human being who was sympathetic to our plight and never let me leave their home without some food.

When we left Plattling, Sorenson instructed me to take along some sewing supplies. After walking a few days and nights we stopped in a barn overnight in a town called Eggenfelden. The next morning Sorenson came by on his two-seater motorcycle to take me with him. He, in his SS uniform, and I in my striped prisoner's uniform, rode across Eggenfelden with people staring at us. It was quite a sight to see a German SS officer and a Jewish prisoner riding together! My immediate task was to repair his civilian clothing, which I surmised he might wear if he ran away. When Sorenson returned me to the barn, everyone was dancing because they had heard rumors that the war was over and Hitler was dead. I had to tell them not to rejoice yet. While in Sorenson's office I heard on the radio that Hitler was very much alive and the war was not yet over. There was no reason to celebrate yet.

We resumed marching again. At one stop, when we were near Mühldorf, we noticed that the German soldiers were very uneasy. Sorenson and the German soldiers were worried that we were surrounded and there was no place to run anymore. A German sentry arrived on a motorcycle and spoke to Sorenson briefly. After their conversation our march resumed. We thought that liberation was at hand, but once again we were disappointed. By then Sorenson had had enough. That night, he ran away, probably wearing the very same suit I had repaired for him. I never saw nor heard from him again.

We arrived in the town of Garching, Germany in the lower Alps on May 3rd and stayed overnight in a barn. How do I know that it was May 3rd? Somehow we learned the date from a newspaper or other source and the date was known to all of us because it's a Polish national holiday. It was snowing that night, but it was not unusual to have snow in the Alps in May. I was with my father, Leon Fruchtman, and my friend, Max Greenberg, who had been Goeth's personal barber in Plaszow and a beautician for Goeth's mistresses. Throughout the death march, my father, Max, Leon and I stayed together giving each other physical and emotional support. Eventually, however, Max became so debilitated and weakened by starvation he couldn't walk anymore. Leon and I supported Max, trying not to let him fall so he would not be left behind. We knew that any prisoner who could not keep up with the group would be shot. After some time, however, a German guard came by and said "Leave him alone. He cannot walk anymore." I replied that we would try to bring him with us, but the guard said that we had to leave him behind because he was holding everyone up. He kept Max behind and we heard shots fired. We realized that we had lost Max. Now we were inconsolable because Max had become another victim. He had endured so much and it was so near to the end of the war. It was another personal tragedy for us.

The following day, a German guard named Frank took my father and me away from the group to be shot.

About two days before we left Plattling, Frank wanted me to make him a pair of pants. I agreed to make them not knowing how soon we'd be leaving, but then the camp closed and I had no time to make them. As a result he threatened to kill my father and me when he had an opportunity. We stood there facing his rifle barrel and all my father could say was, "We tried so hard. We made it this far, but it was not meant to be." It seemed as though the closer we got to the war's end, the closer my father and I were to being killed. After surviving so much, every day seemed to come with another threat to our lives.

A fellow prisoner noticed what was happening and ran to the new commandant who had taken over after Sorenson ran away, and told him that the two tailors were about to be shot. The commandant ran to Frank, screaming from a distance, "Don't shoot." He stated that from now on no one would be killed. He stopped Frank at the very last moment before he pulled the trigger. That was another miracle.

After that incident we continued marching until we reached the town of Trostberg, Germany. In Trostberg they put us on a short train, which was one of the very few trains still running in southern Germany, since most of them had been bombed and destroyed. When I was on the train, some of the Germans put their knapsacks on the steps between the cars and made me guard them. Knowing that the war was ending I could have easily run away, but again, if I ran away my father and many others would likely have paid with their lives for my freedom. I could not have that on my conscience.

When we arrived in Traunstein, Germany later that day, we were sheltered in a barn for the night. We were exhausted. I was sleeping when my father suddenly woke me. It was still dark, in the very early morning hours, when he whispered, “Let’s run away.” After all that we had experienced I thought we could and should take a chance. We couldn’t count on another miracle. So I listened to my father and we ran away with another prisoner. There we were in Traunstein wearing prisoners’ striped uniforms, not knowing where to go or what to do. The war was still not over but we knew that the end was near because we heard explosions all around us, that we had not heard before. We had hardly walked a quarter of a mile when a German sentry stopped us. He asked, “Where are you going?” I was quick enough to say we had been sleeping with a group but they didn’t wake us before they left. We were trying to catch up with them. The German informed us that there was a group that had just gone by. If we walked fast enough we could catch up with them.

We went a little further when we were stopped again by another German sentry who put us in a truck. He spoke to the driver briefly. The driver started to drive away and I asked the driver, “Where are you taking us?” He replied, “I have an order to take you into the woods to kill you, but the war is almost over so get off my truck and run away.” We were afraid, and didn’t know if we could believe him. It was a common practice for German soldiers to shoot their victims in the back when they ran away, so we were worried that that might be his plan. We took a chance, however, and ran as fast as we could, but he never fired his gun. At that point, the other prisoner decided to separate from us and I never saw him again. I know that he survived the war, however, because I heard that from other survivors.

My father and I started walking again. We approached a farm with great trepidation because we did not know what we would find there, but we were in Germany and hiding in the woods was not safe because there were too many German soldiers around. Therefore, we felt we had no choice but to go to the farm. When we opened the farmhouse door the two of us looked at each other, stunned. There were about 50 Germans in air force uniforms sitting at a long table studying maps. Our hearts sank. We couldn't walk away because they had already seen us.

As we entered, a high-ranking officer approached us and asked, "How far away is the front line?" It was interesting that this was his first question and that he had asked us about the front line. I replied I didn't know but it must be very close because we could hear explosions everywhere. He then asked us what we were doing there. I told him the same story that I had previously told the German sentry – we were sleeping when our group left and we were now trying to catch up with them. He also wanted to know if we were hungry and when we replied, "very" he gave us some food. We knew then that they wouldn't kill us.

While we were in the barn we learned from the owner that the previous day an escaping prisoner had been shot by a SS officer who lived next door. Luckily the officer had run away just before we arrived.

It is ironic that we spent the last night of WWII with about 50 German air force deserters waiting for the Americans to liberate all of us. When I woke up the following morning and looked out through the opening in the barn I saw soldiers that looked different from German soldiers. I saw trucks that were different from German army trucks. Just as I had seen swastikas on September 1, 1939, on the low flying planes over my village, now there were no swastikas anywhere – only American flags. I realized that the war was over. We were finally free!

Now, what would happen next?

A photo of me as a 20-year-old liberated, but displaced person, in Germany

Chapter Five
Post-War Adjustments

My father and I left the barn on May 9, 1945. We were finally able to taste freedom. We did not have to worry about a guard walking behind us with a gun on his shoulder, ready to shoot us at any time. Though as wonderful as it was to be free, there was not much else to celebrate. I looked at my father, in his striped prisoner's uniform. He was so pitifully thin and looked so tired. Reality set in. I had no illusions about any of my family members having survived, except perhaps my brother. We realized the enormous losses that we had sustained. Five, and likely six, of us were gone forever. The rage and sorrow of this certainty was overwhelming. We had no home to return to, and no family waiting for us. Where could we go now?

Our only choice was to remain in Germany, our greatest enemy at that time. After thinking about our options, we decided to retrace our steps to Plattling, the site of our last camp. At least there I knew a German baker and a German butcher, whom I had met when I went with a SS man to pick up food for our camp, so I thought that at least we'd have food. Perhaps we would also find a few survivors that we knew. Since there was no vehicular traffic, we started to walk at a slow pace down the middle of the road. We were not alone. There were many nationals from different countries that had been brought to Germany for forced labor and there were many survivors doing what we were doing - wondering, wandering, not knowing where to go or what to do.

As we were walking, an American soldier named Harry Schiff, from a nearby medical unit, stopped us and asked if we were Jewish. When we responded, "Yes," he embraced us. He told us that when he had left his home in America he had promised his parents that when the war was over he would search for Jewish survivors. We were the first that he had encountered. We were overjoyed because he was the first Jewish American serviceman we met. He conversed in broken Yiddish, but the brutality and the horror we expressed was clear to him. Harry was shocked and dismayed listening to our stories. We told him that we were very hungry, so he went to his ambulance, but he returned not with food, but with disinfectants, soaps, lotions and towels. He informed us that getting us cleaned up was first priority; food would come afterward. Not getting food immediately was not easy, but he gave us priceless advice - to eat slowly and sparsely since our digestive systems needed time to readjust. Sadly, too many survivors did not get or heed this advice, and as a result they died shortly after their liberation because they ate too much, too quickly.

We also told Harry that my mother's sister lived in New York, but we did not have her address. He promised that when he returned to the United States he would place an ad in Jewish newspapers with our names and the names of our relatives in New York, hoping that we'd connect. He followed through! My aunt, Bella Stein, read the ad that he placed in the *Forward* newspaper, and then contacted the Joint Distribution Committee (JDC) because it was managing the process of connecting survivors with their relatives. She was able to send me a letter through the JDC and we then began corresponding. Up to this day, I regret that I never took Harry's address to thank him.

After we left Harry, we continued walking toward the town of Trostberg, Germany, which was about a fifteen mile walk. We were exhausted. Along the way, the roads were lined with German civilian onlookers. All they kept saying was "*Wir haben nicht gevust,*" which means "we did not know." None of us said anything to them. We just kept walking. When we finally arrived in Trostberg, a German woman welcomed us into her home. There was no evidence of a man living there, so I assumed that she was a widow. She lived with her younger sister and another young woman about my age. She asked us many questions about our wartime experiences and was very moved and apologetic. I think she was sincerely sorry about what had happened to us. We were able to take baths and after we bathed, she fed us delicious home-cooked food. This, our first real meal since leaving home, was heavenly. Years later, I realized that this wonderful meal was only macaroni and cheese with some meat. Although she gave us some underwear that had belonged to her sister's husband, since we had none during the war years, we were still only able to wear our striped uniforms. After talking to these women for a while, this sympathetic lady gave me a German book titled, *Starker als der Wind*, a story of a young man stranded on an island who survived despite all his challenges. Then she showed us to a bedroom where we were to spend the night - in real beds with real mattresses and real down pillows! It's hard to describe how good that felt after all that we had endured during the past three years. We were ready to remain there forever.

When I woke in the morning, I saw a photo on the dresser of a man in a SS uniform with a medal on his chest. He was the late husband of the younger sister and had lost his life on the Russian front. I was shocked when I realized that I had slept in his bed.

After breakfast, we resumed our walk to Plattling. On the way, there were more survivors walking, and more German civilians lining the roads, saying the same as before, "*Wir haben nicht gevust* - We did not know." Finally, after walking more than fifteen miles, we arrived at the town of Neuötting on the Inn River. We could not continue to Plattling because the bridge had been blown up. We didn't know where to go so we were shown the way to the Town Hall, where the mayor welcomed us and told us of a displaced persons (DP) camp being formed in the nearby sister town of Altötting. We were also given expense money since we had no money whatsoever, and coupons for new clothing, shoes and meals. We spent the night in Neuötting and were assigned a place to stay – a room in a hotel that had been confiscated by the Americans to be used by the survivors, which also had a restaurant. We were given a large room to be shared by five men – my father and I, a Polish man, a Czech man and another Jewish man.

My father only stayed two nights because the following morning a German woman approached him offering him a room in her home. Supposedly, she was anti-Nazi and had few friends in her town. He accepted her invitation and that developed into a friendship that lasted quite a while. The next morning I went to the DP camp in Altötting.

The camp was a large hotel, previously called the Bayericher Hof, that had been confiscated from its Nazi owner and given to the survivors as a DP camp. At the height of the DP camp's existence, there were more than 370 inhabitants. I registered in the camp and was assigned a room, but I was also able to keep a room in Neuötting. My DP camp roommate was Jack (Janek)

Kingsbook, a new-found friend. When I arrived, I was happy to see many of the survivors that I had encountered during the war years. One of the people I reconnected with was my friend, Leon, who had run away from the death march when we had stopped in Trostberg. He hid in the woods until the war's end. Another person I met in the DP camp was Misha Treger, a former lawyer from Kielce, Poland, who later became the director of the camp. Misha and I played chess and checkers on the second day of my arrival. Those were the first games that I had played in many years, but I had not forgotten how to play.

After the second day, we formed a group tasked with collecting bodies of Jewish and Gentile victims who had been shot by the Germans in the nearby fields and woods as the war was ending. It brought back memories of those terrible days in the concentration camps—the stench, the horror—all came back to us as we performed this grizzly task. We collected close to 100 bodies. The American governor forced all of the German administrators to bury these victims in caskets, so that they could have an appropriate funeral and burial. The governor wanted them to see with their own eyes what their country had done. And still, their response was, "*Wir haben nicht gevust* - We did not know."

Our lives while in the DP camp were not easy because we were all focused on finding our families, hoping that they, by some chance, might have survived. In Munich, offices were opened where survivors could go to search for other survivors. The lists were posted daily and changed daily. We all hoped against hope that we would see familiar names on the lists and would find family members and friends who survived. The chances were very slim.

A friend, Ida Greenbaum, learned that her brother, Josef, had survived and supposedly was in Munich. Ida, her boyfriend Leon Fruchtman, who had been with me in Plaszow and on the death march, and I went to Munich to search for him. After numerous inquiries, we learned that he had been in Munich but had already left for Garmisch. We then took a train to Garmisch to search for him. There we learned that he had left for Italy, where groups were forming to go to Palestine illegally. We had no transportation or money so we had to give up our search. It was another five years before Ida was reunited with her brother.

I wanted so much to come up with a plan for myself and get on with my life that when an American Army division was stationed in Neuötting, I opened a sewing factory there, to clean and repair their uniforms. That opportunity gave me additional privileges such as better food and an opportunity to socialize with Americans so that I could learn and practice my English. I also arranged for my friend, Leon Bomchel, a professional baker who stayed with me in Neuötting, to get a job with the American Army. The very same survival skills that I had developed during the war were what I used then to begin to build a new life for myself.

One day, some of us survivors walked by a dancing school. When we heard the music we decided to go in. We approached the owner, an Arthur Murray look-alike, and inquired about lessons. I actually was not in the mood nor did I want to listen to music; however, my companions' wishes prevailed and we went in. The owner asked the musicians to play a march for us. When we heard the music we told him that we didn't intend to listen to any marching music since we had all done enough marching for a lifetime. We left at that point and that was the end of my dancing lessons.

That same night I had a terrifying dream. I dreamt that my friend, Max Greenberg, slapped me in the face and told me that he was sick, in the hospital, and was surprised that I had not come to visit him. When I woke up I had a terrible headache and relived the whole incident of Max being shot and left behind on the death march. I got on my bike, which had been given to me by the Americans, and most likely had been confiscated from the German army. I biked about thirty- five miles to the town where I had been liberated, hoping that the physical exercise would help erase my nightmare.

When I returned to Neuötting that evening, exhausted and disheartened, my father was waiting for me outside my apartment. He was smiling! I asked why he was smiling…whether something had happened…and he exclaimed, "Max is alive!" I laughed and cried all at the same time. When I regained my composure, my father told me that Max was in a hospital in Altötting.

Without skipping a beat, I got back on my bike and rode to Altötting. I arrived at the hospital after visiting hours, but that did not deter me. No one could stop me from visiting Max. After locking up my bike I jumped over the fence. The hospital attendants listened to my story and permitted me to see him despite the late hour.

After tearfully embracing, Max told me what had happened. On that fateful morning on the death march, when he was left behind, a German soldier pushed him into a snow-filled ditch. Max recalled hearing shots, and then blacked-out. He was lying in the ditch the entire day, unconscious, and unaware of his surroundings. When he woke up, it was night and he was cold. He thought, "If I'm cold, I guess I am not dead." He looked and felt for blood and wounds, and was surprised to realize that his body was intact - no blood, nor any wounds. When he tried to stand, however, he could not. He was very wet and chilled from the melting snow, so he crawled on his hands and knees toward a distant light coming from a farmhouse. He finally arrived and knocked on the door. A farmer answered and took him inside his house. The farmer called an ambulance, which took Max to the hospital in Altötting, which was where we were.

Max received the medical attention that he needed and after spending a few months in the hospital, he recovered completely. I stayed in touch with him during his recovery, and after his release Max joined me in the DP camp where he got a job in the office and became involved in the camp's many activities.

In July of 1945, I took a bicycle ride to the DP camp in Altötting and saw an open truck parked in front of the main building. Someone told me that some survivors were returning to Poland so, on the spur of the moment, I decided to join them. I asked my friends, Lena and Genia (Jean) Klein, who were sisters, to hold my bicycle for a few weeks because I was leaving for Poland. I also asked them to tell my father of my plans. I had only the shirt and pants that I was wearing, but I figured I could buy things on the way. We got as far as the Polish border when we heard about survivors who had returned and were killed by Poles. We were shocked to learn of these incidents. The Poles had suffered so much, along with Polish Jews, that you would think they would be sympathetic to the survivors' plight. Unfortunately though, there were some Poles who wanted a Poland free of Jews. They were concerned that the returning survivors would want their homes and personal property back.

It was a very dark period in Polish history and Polish-Jewish relations. Our country was not anxious to welcome us back to the towns and communities from which we had been taken. Fearing for our lives, we never crossed the Polish border. We reversed our course and returned to Altötting. It took me 43 more years before I returned to Poland.

After that attempt to return to Poland, I read an announcement in a German newspaper that Amon Goeth, the former commander of Plaszow, had been arrested by the Americans and was in a prison in Dachau, Germany. The American Army prosecutors were searching for witnesses to his atrocities. Leon, Max and I left for Dachau immediately to testify. When we saw Goeth we were shocked. This murderer who was once the master of life or death was now very thin and stooped over. Goeth denied that he knew who we were, even though Max had been his barber and his mistresses' beautician and saw him regularly, and Goeth had visited our factory often to collect the jewelry and money that had been sewn into prisoners' clothing. We testified against him, which gave us some degree of satisfaction. Eventually he was returned to Poland by the Americans, where he was tried by the Polish authorities, convicted and hung in Krakow on September 13, 1946. His ashes were thrown into the Vistula River.

Years later as I began to conduct research for this book, I found the transcript of Amon Goeth's trial in Poland, which was held in August and September 1946. During the trial he claimed that many inmates at Plaszow had firearms and that many had tried to escape. Most likely he was referring to the Jewish Police Commandant, Wilek Chilowicz, who in fact, he had framed and killed. I was stunned by his response to the prosecutor who asked him how it was possible for firearms to be smuggled into the camp given the high degree of security. Goeth responded that there was a tailoring factory in Plaszow that repaired uniforms for the Germans and other guards. He claimed that among the uniforms sent back for repair, firearms were often smuggled in by the soldiers and Russian guards. That meant that he had suspected all of us who worked in the tailoring factory of having firearms, since we were the only tailoring factory in Plaszow that had direct contact with the guards.

Now I understood why Goeth often peeked through the opening in the factory door! There is no doubt in my mind that had he not been arrested by the Germans in September 1944, we all would have been doomed. Once again, God watched over us.

It took the DP camp inhabitants about three months before they began to resume some semblance of a normal life. We were all anxious to put the war behind us, but it wasn't easy. We formed a very close circle of friends. So many of us had lost family members that Leon and Ida, Janek and Lena, Ben and Genia Krotowski and myself, became each other's "family." We remained very close friends from that time forward.

In the camp, a small restaurant was opened, similar to a coffee shop, where later we even held dances. Couples formed, relationships flourished and weddings were held. The kitchen became a focal point for those events, and the female survivors often cooked in the kitchen, providing home cooked meals for everyone.

My father and Mr. Gdanski, an observant survivor, officiated at these wedding ceremonies since there were no ordained rabbis on site. In the Jewish religion, one does not have to be an ordained rabbi to officiate, and the couples went to the local city hall for their civil marriage certificates. Luckily, someone in our camp had gone to Munich and brought me a printed copy of a *ketubah,* the Jewish wedding contract. I copied that *ketubah* several times and then hand decorated and personalized each one in Hebrew. It was my way of making the occasions special despite the struggles we were still experiencing. Some of those *ketubahs* are still owned by survivors' families.

These weddings were very special events and everyone in the camp participated. We all contributed what we could to make each of the weddings unique. Guests included American soldiers, staff and the camp inhabitants. The brides either had their dresses made by local dressmakers or purchased wedding gowns in town, while the men bought business suits locally. Receptions were held in the hotel, with music played by local German bands, food purchased on the black market and supplemented by the United Nations Relief and Rehabilitation Administration (UNRRA), and lots of wine. Most of the time, I supplied the wine because I knew the wine merchants in Neuötting. My dear friends, Leon and Ida, were the third couple to get married in the camp. It was a joyous and exceptional wedding because many UNRRA representatives and dignitaries attended.

In the fall of 1945, I went to the mess hall for the first day of Rosh Hashanah services. I was stunned to see about 90 percent of the survivors in attendance. We had kippahs (skullcaps), prayer shawls and prayer books supplied by the U.S. Army and UNRRA. Many American soldiers from the surrounding area also attended our services. Following this very emotional service, we survivors shared our feelings. Despite all that we had experienced and endured, we were very thankful to have survived. If not for the help "from above" none of us believed we could have survived. That was my reentry into Jewish religious life.

In due time, people wanted more privacy and started to eat their meals in their own apartments. Other restaurants in the community also became a part of our social scene. Because we were constantly striving to resume somewhat of a normal life, we had outings to visit mountains, lakes, and museums. We went on boat rides, formed sports teams and held sporting events. Soccer, ping pong and biking became part of our daily routine. Our ping pong and soccer teams joined DP camp leagues so we traveled from camp to camp for scheduled competitions. My friend, Leon, a champion ping pong player, won many competitions, while Leon, Max and I were on the soccer team.

We also held many memorial services for Holocaust victims that were arranged by the Jewish Community Center in Munich and the American Army Jewish chaplains. The transportation to the outings mentioned above was sometimes legal and sometimes illegal because gas was rationed and rare. Transportation to the memorial services and the burials, however, was supplied by the German administration.

Sometime in 1947 we received a telegram from the Jewish Central Committee in Munich that my uncle Menasze, my father's brother, had survived the war and was coming to Landshut, Germany, where there was a camp for newly arrived survivors, coming from Russia through Poland. That was the first word I received that a family member had survived!

My uncle had been in the Polish Army at the outbreak of the war and found himself in Russian-occupied Poland with the retreating Polish Army in 1939. The Russians sent him to Siberia where he remained until the end of the war. Much to our surprise he arrived with a female companion whom he had met in Siberia. His first wife, my aunt Sala, died in the Holocaust along with their two children. I gave them my room in Neuötting and I returned to the DP camp. Menasze informed me that my cousin, Abram Fiszler, with whom I had leased an orchard during summers before the war, had also survived in Russia. He too was in a DP camp in Germany. However, by the time I learned that he had already gone to Palestine illegally. As a result I did not get to see Abram until 1983 when I went to Israel for the first time.

In 1947, there was still severe rationing because of the dearth of all kinds of commodities. However, we were able to access many items that could not be found in stores through our various connections in the camp and on the "street." As a result, we became very involved in the black market; the underground economy that was very active in Germany at that time. While living in Neuötting, I got to know many farmers and butchers, so I was able to get eggs, meat, and butter from them…all items which were not easily available legally. In exchange, I paid them with chocolate, cigarettes and coffee which I got from the black market.

While I had access to these things, many of my friends didn't, so I did the purchasing and resold them to friends and acquaintances. And if friends could not afford something, I often gave it to them anyway. Money had little meaning to me at that time. As long as I had enough money for that particular day, I didn't worry about the next day. After what I had witnessed and experienced during the war, money had little significance to me.

There were two movie theaters in town that serviced neighboring communities and there were often long lines for both. Because we were survivors, and because I knew the owners of both theaters, I was able to purchase tickets in advance and distribute them to my DP camp friends. After having stood in line for innumerable roll calls in the various concentration camps, we all vowed that we would never stand in line again.

In mid-to-late 1947, a post war Zionist Convention was held in Munich. At that time, the United Nations was debating the question of partitioning Palestine. Would the Jewish people have an independent state? A woman, Edka Blaimanowa, and I were elected to represent our DP camp at this Convention. That event had a lasting impact on me. On the opening night we convened in a German theater where Hitler used to meet with his associates. Beryl Locker, a representative to the UN from the Jewish Agency in Palestine, stopped at the Convention prior to returning to Palestine, and was the keynote speaker. You could hear a pin drop during the entire two hour presentation. At the closing, the entire Convention audience rose to sing *Hatikvah*, which later became the Israeli national anthem. There was not a dry eye among all the participants. How ironic, that we were meeting in a place where our enemies planned our extinction, but we survived despite their efforts and were making plans for our future. Our determination to build something new and move on was clearly evident that evening.

On the third day of the Convention we heard from survivors who had been on the *Exodus*. This was the ship carrying more than 4,000 Jewish displaced persons to Palestine, which had been intercepted by the English Navy and forced to return to Europe. Initially, they were taken to France, from where they had embarked, but the French authorities said they would only allow the passengers to disembark if they did so voluntarily and the passengers refused to get off the ship. Consequently, after three weeks, the British brought the displaced persons to Hamburg, Germany, where they were then held in Britsh-administered detention camps. After hearing their stories, we closed the doors, spread fabric on the stage, and collected money and jewelry for the Haganah, the underground Jewish army that later became the Israel Defense Forces. Watches, chains, rings, bracelets, ear-rings, money - anything of value was thrown onto the fabric. The sight of that emotional outpouring is still with me today.

When we returned from the Convention, we learned that some of our friends had received their U.S. immigration papers. Among that group were my friends, Leon and Ida, who as mentioned earlier, were the third couple to marry in the DP camp. However, even though they got their official papers, it would take some time before they could leave since they had to get physical exams and wait for the ship to take them to their new lives.

In November 1947, after the UN General Assembly passed a resolution to partition Palestine into a Jewish state and an Arab state, the DP camp population diminished. Many of my close friends decided to emigrate to Palestine despite the dangers they would likely face there. At that time, the only way to enter Palestine, was through the Aliyah Bet, which is the Hebrew name given to the clandestine immigration of Jews to Palestine before Israel was established. Many survivors who tried to get to Palestine, however, were detained in Cyprus by the English military, which strictly limited and even forbade Jewish immigration to Palestine because they did not want to antagonize the Arabs. Other survivors emigrated to Australia where immigration was legal, and some went to Canada, which had less restrictive immigration laws than the United States, where strict immigration quotas limited the ability of Holocaust survivors to enter. A few lucky ones were able to emigrate to the U.S. because their relatives sponsored them or they had young children, which gave them preference. Astonishingly, it was actually easier for German citizens to immigrate to the U.S. at that time, than it was for Jewish survivors!

With each passing day, life in the DP camp grew more stifling. Each of us wanted to move on with our lives, but we were in limbo. While we waited for our papers, my father found a new companion who lived in Rosenheim, Germany, a small city about forty miles outside of Munich. Through this relationship, he met an Italian man with whom he formed many business connections in Rosenheim. One of the people he met was Sholek Kesten, another survivor, who became a lifelong friend. Eventually, since my father spent so much time in Rosenheim, he decided to move there permanently, and remained there for the rest of his life. I visited him there often and throughout the years he and Sholek Kesten celebrated many Shabbats and Jewish holidays together.

In the interim, to keep myself busy and to break the daily boredom, I opened a convenience store in the camp and I started to learn English formally from a German woman to prepare for my eventual emigration to the United States. My friend Lena joined me twice a week for those lessons in Neuötting. Our teacher befriended Lena, and was instrumental in getting her relatives in California to sponsor Lena and her husband, Janek Kingsbook. Lena had read a book about California while in the DP camp, and it became the place she dreamed of emigrating to. Eventually, her dreams came true!

On May 14, 1948, David Ben-Gurion, Israel's first prime minister, proclaimed the establishment of the Jewish state – the State of Israel. We were ecstatic and were singing and dancing in the streets. Sadly, however, the next day five Arab nations - Egypt, Syria, Jordan, Lebanon and Iraq - attacked Israel. Most of the survivors, who had arrived clandestinely in Palestine, joined the Israeli Army and fought in the War of Independence.

I did not receive my immigration papers to the United States until May 1949, and unfortunately my father's papers were delayed. A clerical error turned out to be a life-changing event for us. Had we received our papers at the same time, most likely he would have come with me to the U.S., but his papers didn't arrive for another four to five months. By that time, my father had opened a jewelry and clothing business in Rosenheim which was doing well. He was very concerned about starting all over again in a new country, with a new language, new environment, having to start a new business, and having to face new challenges, so he chose to remain in Germany. His lifestyle suited him, but for me there was no future in Germany.

Before leaving Germany, I reflected on my four years spent there. I had no responsibilities. I worked whenever I felt it necessary, and I played whenever I wanted to. I had made many friends, Jewish and Gentile. I had many German friends and realized that not all Germans were guilty, especially the younger ones. There were many times when I was having a good time that I asked myself, 'Should I be enjoying myself when my family was destroyed under such horrific conditions?' My lifestyle, though, was unrealistic and it was time for me to move on to begin a new life. I knew that I could never forget my past, but that I had to try to begin again. I was leaving my father behind, my only surviving family member. Even though we did not live together, we both knew that we were there for each other. Now we were going to be separated by thousands of miles. Had the war not happened, our lives would have been very different.

With all those thoughts on my mind, in July 1949, I boarded a train to Bremen, Germany not knowing what the future held. I was alone and about to begin a new life in a foreign country. There was no looking back. I was 24 years old.

Chapter Six Life Begins Anew in America

In mid-July 1949, along with about 1,200 very excited and very nervous Holocaust survivors, we left Bremen, Germany for America, aboard the USS General R. L. Howze (AP-134), a vessel that had been a US army transport. Finally, we were on our way to a new land and a new life. Because this ship was a former military transport vessel, the living accommodations were not particularly glamorous. The men and women were housed separately in dormitories of about 500, sleeping in three tier bunks. That was not too different from what we had had in our former concentration camps except that these bunks had mattresses. There were a few toddlers on board who had been born in the DP camps so they were housed with their mothers. Despite the eerily similar sleeping quarters, this time we slept easier. We had nothing to fear. The American crew was very kind, helpful and compassionate.

As we made our way across the ocean from our old world to our new world, we encountered a severe storm. Luckily I was one of the very few passengers that did not get seasick. One of the couples that I had befriended in the DP camp had a young child, so I went to the women's dormitory to see how they were faring. What I encountered there was quite an awful scene. All of the women were very ill, nauseous and exhausted from motion sickness. In the midst of all that misery I called out repeatedly to my friend. When she finally answered, I heard more of a groan from her than something that resembled actual speech. With some difficulty, I was able to get her up on deck so that the fresh air could revive her. A crew member gave me an orange for her, and the combination of fresh air and fresh fruit did the trick. Eventually the storm subsided, and we continued on our way. The crossing from then on was rather uneventful. The passengers were now focused on what was waiting for them on the other side of the ocean. There was a positive and negative tension in the air. Some of us were so excited, we couldn't wait to begin a new life, while others were more wary of what awaited them when we docked in America.

My English was limited, but better than most of the survivors on board, so I was able to converse with the crew. They elected me to be the ship announcer so that I could keep the passengers informed. During the crossing, they had me address the survivors as immigrants. On the next to the last day of our trip I greeted everyone as "future American citizens" which was met with tremendous cheers. After eleven days at sea, we arrived at a Manhattan pier, late on a Thursday night. It was too late to disembark so we remained on deck all night, curiously watching the passing cars on the New Jersey coastline and the twinkling lights in the distance. Despite the uncertainty we faced, for just this night I was that same 14-year-old boy sitting on my window sill staring into the stars and dreaming about my future. It was a melancholy moment in time. I wasn't that young boy any longer. My youth had been snatched away from me by what I had experienced during the war. I had seen too much to ever view the stars with such innocence and pure joy again.

My first impression of America though, was awe and wonder. The non-stop sound and light show of cars was mesmerizing and made me wonder if anyone slept here. Presiding over this spectacle was the majestic Statue of Liberty. We had all seen pictures and heard of this landmark, but no words or pictures could do her justice. We knew that the sight of Lady Liberty actually greeting us meant our nightmare was over!

The following morning I was greeted by my cousin Harry Stein, my Aunt Bella's son, and my friend, Ben, who had arrived in America a few months earlier. Harry learned of my survival by reading a Jewish newspaper that listed survivors searching for family. Harry Schiff, the American soldier that I met on the day of my liberation, had listed my name. He had promised me he would do it, and he did! After greeting me, Ben returned to his home in Manhattan and I continued on my journey to Williamsburg, Brooklyn with my new-found cousin. We drove through garbage-strewn Delancey Street in Lower Manhattan on a hot July Friday afternoon. This was not what I thought New York would look or smell like. That scene and the accompanying smells did not make a very good first impression. However, as we continued on to Brooklyn, the scenery improved and I was more and more anxious to embrace a family I had never met before. What were they like, I wondered? Would I fit in?

Meeting my mother's sister, Bella, and her other children, Herbert and Rose, was the culmination of one of the dreams I had in my darkest days during the war. I was the first European family member that Bella had seen in over 30 years. Hugging her – my mother's sister – was very emotional. I realized I had no reason to be anxious because I now had family members who embraced me tearfully and warmly. They showered me with love, and asked too many questions about the family members that we had lost. I told them as much as I could, but telling them everything at that time was impossible. It was too raw and brutal for me to dredge up. I wanted to leave all of those questions in the past. I did what I could to explain, but some of their questions were impossible to answer. How could my father and I survive, when others did not? That question haunted all of us then and even now continues to be "the elephant in the room" for survivors like me. There is no explanation that makes sense at all to any of us who managed to live through those terrible years.

Prior to dinner that evening, I was invited into a neighbor's apartment to watch television, which for me was a first. I had heard about television but couldn't imagine how it worked. It was a very hot and humid afternoon and when I arrived at his apartment, the neighbor who was very short and had high blood pressure, was sitting shirtless in a stuffed armchair looking at the TV and straining to see something on a very small screen. He had what looked like an ice compress on his head. It was a curious sight. I put two and two together and came to the conclusion that if you watch television, you need to use an ice compress. That was my introduction to TV. It was the first of many glorious and wondrous things to experience in America.

Having arrived on a Friday meant that that evening I had a traditional Shabbat dinner; the first I had with family since I had left home in 1942. Candles were lit, Shabbat prayers were chanted, and I feasted on chicken soup, gefilte fish, roast chicken and all the other traditional foods that I had not had since 1942.

Following that Shabbat dinner, my relatives invited many neighbors, mostly young single women, to meet me, especially since I was also single. I spoke English, was young, reasonably good looking, and unattached, but I also was not interested. Additionally, I had no money. As I stated earlier, I learned during the war that having money made no difference as to whether one lived or died. While in the DP camp I helped friends who were struggling financially, but I lived from day to day, happy knowing that I had enough money for that day, and I'd worry about tomorrow, tomorrow. I had confidence and knew that I could always make money. This outlook and attitude, however, did not make me a very good candidate for a prospective husband. Besides, why should I settle down when I had a clean slate of life before me?

I now had family, food and freedom, but I realized that my new-found family was much more observant than I was. I had not experienced that level of religiosity since I left home. I felt like a fish out of water in some ways. At the same time, at the dinner table I had sensed that some of my cousins were not so observant. So, after the parade of single women, I suggested that we go for a walk to get some fresh air. This evening "walk" took us to Times Square, which dazzled me to no end. This was the New York that I had seen in movies and photos. I was hooked.

The next day, after attending morning services at a local synagogue, I traveled to Manhattan to visit friends living on 84th Street and Amsterdam Avenue. I decided to stay overnight because the New York scene was so exhilarating. I did not want to miss any of what it had to offer. Little did I know that ambulance sirens blaring all night long would not let me sleep, so that too was a side of Manhattan that I did not expect. I was now in the middle of the hustle and bustle I was first exposed to while docked in New York Harbor. My introduction to Manhattan was an incessant symphony of cars, subways and sirens, and I was captivated by it.

The following day I visited the offices of the *Aufbau*, a German Jewish newspaper popular with the survivor population. Since I was a passionate soccer player and follower, they assigned me to their soccer team, and on my first Sunday in America, I played soccer in 97 degree heat for the New World Club in Van Cortlandt Park. I was not accustomed to that kind of heat and humidity, but I know that I played well because I overheard some German Jewish spectators comment, "Look how well that Polish Jew plays."

On Monday I went to the Joint Distribution Committee (JDC) office for assistance in finding work. They sent me to the Men's Clothing Union, which in turn sent me to a few garment center factories. One of them was a furrier. Three survivors, including me, were given fur trimmings to add to garments as a test to see how skilled we were. At the end of the day, the owner said that he could only retain one of us because his factory was so small. He offered me the job but I told him that the other two men needed the job more than I did, so I left. The next day I went to a coat factory on Nostrand Avenue in Brooklyn. There too, there were a few of us trying out for the same job. We were each given some coats to assemble. At the end of the day I had made only one coat while the others had made about five or six each. I was therefore surprised when the owner offered me the job. His explanation was that my coat really looked like a coat while the others did not! That one job launched my career in the garment industry.

In a few weeks, the owner became ill and his doctor advised him to take a vacation in Florida to recover. He delegated the responsibility of managing the factory to me. That was my lucky break! I worked hard to make the most of it. All the businesses that I dealt with were very satisfied with our finished garments, and the factory workers lavished me with gifts because since I had taken over, they had never made so much money in that season. When the owner returned, he was very pleased with what I had done in his absence. As a result, a Manhattan coat manufacturer, with whom he did business, offered me a job as his production manager. I was a quick learner and not afraid of taking on more responsibility. I remained on that job for twelve years. I was well on my way now. I became very independent and made a good income. Those years gave me a solid footing in the garment industry, as well as in New York, my adopted home. Those experiences also prepared me for opening my own business, to contract and manufacture women's coats and suits.

I continued to live with my Aunt Bella for quite a while before deciding that it was time to strike out on my own. My aunt was Orthodox and expected that I would also be observant, but I was not. It was uncomfortable for both of us since we were not of the same mindset with regard to religious practices. I felt like I was disappointing her, but I couldn't change for her. I found a studio apartment on 92nd Street and 2nd Avenue, bought a Castro Convertible sofa and other basic furnishings to make it my home, and I became a happy resident of Manhattan.

My original plan when I came to the United States was to continue my education. I was not sure what I wanted to study but thought that I should further my schooling. Some of the schools that I applied to found my English inadequate, while others found me over qualified. In the meantime, I had a good job, was making a good salary and having a great social life. So little by little, additional schooling became less of a priority.

My English was improving daily because I read newspapers and books a great deal, and I socialized primarily with Americans. Life, in general, was sweet. Working in the garment industry gave me easy access to lots of beautiful single women, so my social life was very active. I was enjoying my bachelorhood and making up for lost time, sowing my wild oats.

In the meantime, my European friends were moving on with their lives. Leon and Ida moved to Philadelphia where Leon had relatives who had sponsored them. Max had moved to Springfield, Massachusetts where he had a sponsor and he was now married to Dorothy. Both Leon and Max had children who became like my nieces and nephews.

My lifestyle was very different from my friends. I was "the man about town" while they now had the responsibilities that go along with marriage and fatherhood. I was not quite ready for that - nor did I know if I ever would be - but I always made time to share birthdays, anniversaries and other happy events with them. They were my extended family.

A few months after I was living in my own apartment, my father came for a visit because his immigration papers had finally come through. I was working full time so he was on his own during the day. After spending much time investigating what life was like in Manhattan, he decided that he was too old to make another drastic change in his life. He had settled in Rosenheim, Germany where he had already established a successful business. The German government was generous and compassionate to survivors, so he had a very decent quality of life. The thought of learning a new language, starting a new business, and starting over again was too overwhelming, so he decided to return to Germany. That disappointed and troubled me, but through the years, he often visited me in the U.S., and I made annual trips to Germany to visit him. Sometimes I would spend up to six weeks with him. We both preferred to look forward and not talk about the past, so we rarely talked about our wartime experiences because it was too painful.

Back in America, my life was full. I got great satisfaction from my work and I had an active social life, but I began to realize that all this socializing was not very satisfying. While I thoroughly enjoyed the Manhattan nightlife - the nightclubs and restaurants, especially the Copacabana and the Balalaika - and I had plenty of dates, there was an emptiness to my life. Perhaps it was time to think about settling down.

On one occasion when I visited Max in Springfield, Massachusetts a co-worker of his gave him a phone number to give me. It was the number of her sister-in-law's sister, Rhoda, who was living and teaching in the Hartford, Connecticut area. I put it in my pocket where it stayed until I returned to Springfield for Max's son's bris. There I met the sister and brother-in-law of the mystery woman whose phone number I couldn't seem to throw away. I liked them immediately. When I returned home, I retrieved the phone number and decided to call her. When I called, she was less than enthusiastic. I spoke with a decided accent; I had no car which meant that I would have to travel by train to Hartford, and I would have to stay overnight in a hotel. She felt that this was just too much for a blind date, and turned me down! I have always been persistent, so I called again and was met with pretty much the same response.

Not to be deterred, I tried again. Realizing that I would not accept "no" for an answer, she agreed to go out with me but enlisted her roommate, Hermia, and Hermia's new boy-friend, Arnie, to double date with us. When I arrived in Hartford, I realized that I only had Rhoda's phone number and not her address, so I had to call Rhoda to get her address. That was not a good start and hardly the way to impress a date! That evening, the four of us went to Bradley Field, a very popular place at the time, for dinner and dancing. The evening lasted well into the wee hours of the morning...and the rest is history.

Not long afterward, I met Rhoda's parents who lived in North Adams, Massachusetts in the Berkshires. Both of her parents were born in Europe and I immediately felt a close connection to them. They were wonderful people and reminded me of the people from my hometown in Poland. Rhoda's father had come to America when he was 16 years old to avoid being conscripted into the Czar's army for 25 years. Sadly, his family remained in Russia and perished in the Holocaust. He had been in touch with them until the beginning of the war, but then all communications stopped.

I also met Rhoda's four brothers, got reacquainted with her sister, Sunny, and met her many aunts and uncles, most of whom lived in Manhattan. Their living in Manhattan made it very convenient for me since Rhoda could travel back and forth from Manhattan and stay with them when I was not able to visit her in Connecticut. We met in November 1957 and got married in North Adams on August 3, 1958, the happiest day of my life. Rhoda left her teaching job and moved to Manhattan, sharing my studio apartment on East 92nd Street. With her parents, siblings, aunts and uncles, I once again had a large family. Oh how I wished that I could have shared this day with the loved ones that I had lost, but I faced reality. I was determined to move on and not look back. I promised myself that with this new beginning I would not ask my wife to confront the horrors of the Holocaust. Nightmares still haunted me, but I promised myself that I would not inflict this on anyone else. That was not easy, but again, I was determined to look forward and move on with my life. And move on, we did.

We moved to Forest Hills, Queens where we lived for five years. While living there our son, David, was born on February 17, 1962. Then when Rhoda was expecting again and we needed more space, we moved to Kew Gardens, Queens where our daughter, Laura, was born on December 24, 1964. During that period, my father came for extended stays so that he got to know his grandchildren and they got to know him. Despite the language barrier, they communicated beautifully. We also traveled to Germany twice with David and Laura, when they were in elementary school, so that they could get to know their grandfather better. Again, they had no problem communicating with him. Love and laughter break many barriers. What a joy it must have been for my father to know that our family would continue after he was gone.

In 1969, when Laura was ready to enter kindergarten, there was a major teacher's strike in New York City, so we decided to move to the suburbs. We bought a lovely colonial home in Rockville Centre, New York, which is in Nassau County on Long Island. That was our home for 36 years. Our years in Rockville Centre were happy and full ones.

Both Rhoda and I were very involved in the community and in our synagogue, Temple B'nai Sholom, where David and Laura attended Hebrew school, and David celebrated his Bar Mitzvah. The children attended Covert Elementary School and graduated from South Side High School. Both David and Laura graduated from the University of Massachusetts in Amherst, as had Rhoda many years before. Both also married while we lived in Rockville Centre. David's marriage, which unfortunately later ended in divorce, blessed us with our first two grandchildren, Brian and Melissa. Laura's marriage to Ronen Wilk, whose father incidentally is also a survivor of Plaszow, blessed us with two grandchildren, Ariel and Daniel. With the birth of my grandchildren I now know how my father felt when he was with my children. After leaving Rockville Centre in 2005, Rhoda and I moved to Wayne, New Jersey, to be closer to Laura and her family.

In 1988, with our children out of college and on their own, we decided to return to Poland and my hometown, Kazimierza Wielka. It was my first time going back since I had left there in 1942. I thought that it was important to share my roots with Rhoda. I knew that it would be a painful trip for me, but I also felt that it was important to do for many reasons. We visited my former school, which had hardly changed. That was the place where I had spent my formative years, but also the place that served as a type of prison for the Jews of Kazimierza Wielka during the liquidation of the Jewish community. I had always told Rhoda and my children that I had to walk a very long distance through snow and sleet to get to school. Consequently, when Rhoda and I got in the car to drive from the school to my former home, I was prepared to drive for a while; what a surprise it was when we arrived there within a few minutes. It was not much more than around the corner!

Many of the stories I had shared with Rhoda came to life on that trip and we had many unique experiences. Word spread quickly throughout Kazimierza Wielka that a survivor had returned. People, some of whom I recognized, and others that I did not, thanked me profusely for what our family had done for theirs. During the battle on September 7, 1939, they found shelter in our brick home, while their wooden homes were threatened. This was now the next generation, but the story had been handed down because they remembered what the Fiszler family had done for theirs. I was moved by their words and happy that my family had achieved some legacy in my hometown.

I visited my first grade teacher, Mrs. Podgurska, who was now quite elderly. I remembered her as a beautiful young woman who introduced me to the world of secular education. She was now well into her 80's and very poor. Her clothing and apartment were threadbare, but she was a most gracious hostess. It was obvious that food and money were scarce, but she offered us bread and butter and tea. I recall looking at Rhoda, wondering if we should be taking food from her, knowing that this was perhaps all she had.

Mrs. Podgurska and I did a lot of reminiscing about my former classmates and members of the Jewish community. She gave me a photograph of our former *beit midrash* that she had taken just before it was destroyed. She was the one who had told me that people from our town dug under it hoping to find treasures buried there. Then she asked me to take her to the burial site in the woods where so many of my family and friends were shot. She wanted to pay her respects to those poor souls. It was a bleak day when we drove to the place in the woods, hidden from the road. There was a small monument there which had been placed there by a survivor from Canada. We wept, said our prayers and left in silence. That was the last time that I saw Mrs. Podgurska. She died the following year.

One of my objectives on that memorable trip was to see if I could find any family photographs. The only photo I have is of my cousin, Mania Morawiecka, which my Aunt Bella gave to me. I have no other pictures of my family and I hoped that perhaps neighbors or friends had some. Not surprisingly, I could not find any, but I did get the surprise of my life when my former landlady invited us into her apartment and presented me with a brass candlestick that had belonged to our family, which my mother had used on every Shabbat and every holiday. Our former landlady kept this precious object hoping that someone in our family had survived and would return someday. This candlestick now resides in our home and is the only tangible evidence I have of my life, with my family, in Poland.

I am a lucky man. Rhoda and I have traveled extensively, including making many trips to Israel where I reconnected with cousins who had survived the war and immigrated there following their liberation. They too were resilient and built new lives – they had families and were successful in business. They have often visited us in the U.S., and we have often visited them in Israel. They also warmly welcomed Laura, and opened their homes to her, when she spent her junior year of college studying at the Hebrew University in Jerusalem.

Zachor-remember. This has become my mission. I grab every opportunity that comes my way to share my history so that the Holocaust is not forgotten. One day, in the not too distant future, there will be no survivors to tell their stories, so it is imperative that I, and others like me, share their Holocaust experiences so that no one can ever doubt that the Holocaust happened. My goal is to educate students, and all whom I encounter, so that they in turn will educate others. The history of the Holocaust must not die when survivors are not here to tell first-hand what happened during that terrible chapter in history. To me, it is still unbelievable and inconceivable that these horrific crimes were committed by civilized nations in the 20th century.

I have participated in nine March of the Living events. This is an annual educational program for students, and recently adults, from all over the world who travel to Poland for a week to learn about the Holocaust and then continue on to the miraculous Jewish State of Israel for another week. During that time they study the history of the Holocaust, and examine the roots of prejudice, intolerance and hate. They visit many Jewish historical sites as well as many concentration and death camps in Poland. When they continue on to Israel, the gloom is replaced with sunshine. In Israel they learn its history, visit many historical sites and just have a great time basking in the light and glory of that amazing country. I have accompanied groups from Long Island and New Jersey as a Holocaust educator, sharing my stories of Jewish life before and during World War II. In 2011, my wife, our cousins Patti and Jim Kronick, and some members of our synagogue, Shomrei Torah in Wayne, NJ, went with me, which was a transforming event for them. In the following years, I was lucky again. My son, David, and grandson Brian, joined me in Poland for part of the event, and the following year my granddaughter, Melissa, also joined me for part of the week in Poland. Laura, our daughter, had traveled with us to Poland on one of our earlier return visits, so now everyone in my immediate family, excluding our younger grandsons, has been to my hometown. Laura's husband, Ronen, has also gone to Poland with his father and three brothers, to learn about his father's experiences during the war.

On each of my visits to Poland, I spend time with Mr. Sikorski's two daughters, his grandson and his grandson's family. They know all about me and my family, and the role that their family played in saving me during the Holocaust. During the war, Mr. Sikorski had been a member of the Polish underground and the AK, which is comparable to our National Guard. Following the war, I tried to stay in touch with him, but he was an ardent anti-Communist when the Communists were in control of the government, and my letters to him were censored. Therefore, it became "uncomfortable" for him to continue our correspondence. Tragically, this noble man - who risked his life and the lives of his family members to hide my sister and me - died in a Communist prison.

From the time of my arrival in the U.S. in 1949, until my father died in 1972, I made almost yearly trips to Germany to visit my father. He had had leukemia for many years and eventually lost his battle against that horrible disease. I was at his bedside at the last moment. This man who had endured so much, fought for his life to the very end. His death was a terrible blow to me because he was my last link to my family. He is buried in a very old, and still functioning, Jewish cemetery in Munich that strangely, was untouched by the war. We have visited his grave many times through the years, with the most recent visit being in 2013.

In 2008, in honor of my 83rd birthday, my wife surprised me with the news that she was planning a second bar mitzvah for me. The Bible says that a normal life span is 70 years, and every year after that is a gift. So since I was now 83, it was time for us to celebrate with a second bar mitzvah. This time, I did not have to go to Hebrew school to learn how to read from the Torah, nor was I nervous. Many loving members of my family and lots and lots of friends, including many that had traveled with me to Poland, shared this memorable time with me. The food was far better and more plentiful than at my first bar mitzvah in 1938, but the connection of this event to my past was not lost on me. In a way, my life had come full circle. Who would have thought that I would live to have this experience?

I have always been extremely grateful for what I have and what I have achieved. I take nothing for granted. I know that each minute is precious, and that each member of my family is even more precious. My wife, Rhoda, my children, David and Laura, their children, Brian and Melissa, and Ariel and Daniel, and Laura's husband, Ronen, have given me more pleasure than I could ever have imagined. They have enabled me to live a very fulfilling and rich life. I am blessed!

I wrote this book for my children, grandchildren and future generations to remember the Holocaust, and never forget what happened to the millions of innocent men, women and children that were killed by the Nazis… perhaps your relatives and ancestors were among them. I hope that my story, and others like mine, will prevent tragedies like the Holocaust from ever happening again.

EPILOGUE

The March of the Living

In an effort to keep the memory of my loved ones alive, I would like to share with you some additional information about my family and some of the individuals mentioned in this book.

Family:

My mother, Rachel, my brothers, David and Moshe, and my sister, Leah, were taken away on a transport in November 1942, and were never heard from again. Based upon research I've conducted, I believe they were likely taken to the Belzec extermination camp and perished there.

My brother, Mendel, was taken on a transport from the Plaszow concentration camp in 1944, and I never saw nor heard from him again. It was not until after the Red Cross' International Tracing Service archives opened in Bad Arolsen, Germany in 2007, that I learned that Mendel died on April 10, 1945, in a hospital in the Flossenbürg concentration camp. The irony is that he was in that camp at the same time or a week before or after my father and I arrived there. Oh how I wish I had known that he was there. I learned that he had worked in a munitions factory in the Sudetan Mountains and never really had a chance. Nearly everyone who worked there was worked to death. He died just one month before the war ended. That was an incredible blow to me.

My mother (Rachel Katz Fiszler) had four sisters and one brother:

> Sister: Feigle Katz (married to Benem Morawiecki). They perished in the Holocaust, along with their six children.
>
> Sister: Leah Katz (married to Isor Fiszler). They had three sons, Zajda, Moshe and Kune. They all perished in the Holocaust.
>
> Sister: Beila (Balche) Katz (married to David Fiszler, my father's brother). They perished in the Holocaust, along with their two children.
>
> Brother: Alter Katz. He died at the beginning of WWII of natural causes. His wife, Pola, and their two children perished in the Holocaust.
>
> Sister: Bella Stein. My mother's sister who had moved to the United States before the war,

sponsored me to come to the United States. She died in the late 1970s/early 1980s.

My father (Selig Fiszler) had four brothers and one sister:

Brother: Pinkus Fiszler. He perished in the Holocaust, along with his wife and six children.

Brother: Josef Fiszler. He perished in the Holocaust, along with his wife and five children. One son, Abram Fiszler, survived (see below).

Brother: David Fiszler (married to my mother's sister, Beila (Balche) Katz). They perished in the Holocaust, along with their two children.

Brother: Menasze Fiszler. He survived WWII and moved to Palestine/Israel.

Sister: Nicha Fiszler (married Yechiel Markowitz). She died at the beginning of the war. Two of their sons, Abram and Mendel Markowitz, survived the war and lived in Palestine/Israel. Abram died about 10 years ago, and I am still in touch with Mendel and with Abram's wife, Dora, and his children, Nachama (Merla) and Yechiel.

Abram Fiszler – my cousin (my uncle Josef's son) with whom I rented an orchard during two summers, survived the war in Russia and moved to Palestine after the war. I first saw him when I visited Israel for the first time in the 1980s, and we saw each other several times after that. He died about 15 years ago.

Mania Morawiecka – my cousin who intended to go to America before the war, perished in the Holocaust.

Moniek Singer – my sister Sarah's husband, was taken away on a transport from Plaszow concentration camp and was never heard from him again.

Other People Mentioned in the Book:

Jozef Rakowski – who was co-president of the Jewish community in Kazimierza Wielka along with my father, survived the war and lived in Ohio. He has since died, but I am in close touch with his son, Sam (Shmuel) Ron, with whom I attended school in Kazimierza Wielka. He is the only survivor of my childhood friends from Kazimierza Wielka. Sam moved to Palestine after the war, where he married Bilha. They now live in Florida.

Roman Sikorski – the Polish man who hid my sister and me and aided my father and brother, when the Germans liquidated our town, had a very tragic life after WWII. He was imprisoned by the Communist regime which had records of his involvement in the Polish-Soviet War in 1920, and sadly he committed suicide while in prison. I was in touch with his wife, Lola Sikorska, but she died quite a few years ago. I remain in close touch with his two daughters, Musia and Romana, his grandson, Piotr and Piotr's wife, Kasia, and their children. I have visited them several times in Poland. They are all just as nice and as good as Roman Sikorski was!

Izia Rutkowska – my friend, whose uncle, Roman Sikorski, hid my sister and me, I saw just once after the war. She was the one who saw my mother being taken away in a transport and told me that my mother cried when passing the hiding place where my sister and I were.

Mrs. Niewiadomska – Roman Sikorski's aunt, died after the war. Sadly, I never saw her after I left my hiding place in 1942.

Mrs. Podgurska – my first grade teacher who took a picture of the *beit midrash* in Kazimierza Wielka before it was destroyed, and gave me the picture when I first visited Poland in 1988, died the following year, in 1989.

Leon Fruchtman – as noted in the book, married Ida Greenbaum in the Altötting DP camp. They had three sons, Eric (married to Vicki), Mark (married to Cheryl) and David (married to Samantha). Leon and Ida lived into their eighties and I stayed in close touch with them over the years…our friendship bound by so many memories of the war and the DP camp. I am still in touch with their sons and their families.

Max Greenberg, married Dorothy, and lived in Springfield, Massachusetts. They had two children, Helene and Mark. Sadly, Max died in the 1970s and I lost touch with his family.

Janek Kingsbook married Lena Klein and they lived in California. Janek has died, but I am still in touch with Lena.

Ben Krotowski married Genia (Jean) Klein, Lena's sister. They later divorced and I only briefly stayed in touch with Jean.

Harry Stein – my cousin who met me when I arrived in NY, is now 93 years old. I am in touch with him, his wife and children.

Herbert and Rose Stein – my cousins, who were my Aunt Bella's children, and I were in close touch, but sadly they have since died.

About This Book and the Sanctity of Life

I wrote this book to fulfill a promise I made to my mother that if I survived, I would tell the world what happened to us simply because we were Jews. Decades passed before I could begin because it was a very emotional experience that resulted in many sleepless nights. As the number of survivors alive to tell their stories is dwindling, I felt compelled to write my story for my children, grandchildren and for future generations so that they could learn what happened to me, my family and countless others.

We Holocaust survivors lived a hell on earth for too many years. We witnessed unspeakable horrors and suffering. We lost our families, our homes, our countries, our opportunities to earn a livelihood, our educations, and along with that, our past. Many survivors, like me, have no photographs of their families or of the lives they lived before the war. The Nazis tried to erase that. Too many innocent people – men, women and children – lost their lives. This memoir, in some small way, seeks to give them a voice and a place in history. I feel that it is my obligation to speak for them.

The story of the Jews during the Holocaust is a story about what happens when bystanders and witnesses to evil do not intercede; that includes governments as well as individuals. I hope my story is a call to action. When you see or know of wrongdoing being done, you must speak up and intervene. Evil thrives on weakness and complacency.

Can I forgive? That is a question that all survivors have been asked. I cannot forgive those that perpetrated the unspeakable crimes committed during the Holocaust. Too many of those war criminals did not pay any price for their crimes and went on to live their lives as free men and women.

Many people ask me about the role of the Polish people during World War II. Were they not as evil as the Nazis? The Nazis built many of their concentration and extermination camps on Polish soil. That, however, was a Nazi decision, not a Polish one. Yes, there were far too many Polish citizens who were informers and revealed hiding places of Jews, resulting in too many of their deaths. There were also some Polish citizens who, either along with the Nazis, or on their own, also committed unspeakable crimes against the Jews. But on the Avenue of Righteous Gentiles at Yad Vashem – the Holocaust memorial museum in Jerusalem, Israel – recognition and thanks is also given to Polish citizens who risked their lives and the lives of their family members to save Jews during WWII. As noted in this book, I would not be here if it were not for Mr. Roman Sikorski, a Polish Gentile, who risked his life and the lives of his family, to aid my sister, my father, my brother and me.

You must consider what you would do if someone asked for your help, knowing that if you did help you would be putting your life and the lives of your family members at risk. I think we all know what we should do, but could we? That is the dilemma that the Polish people were faced with, and many in fact, did pay with their lives for choosing to do the right thing.

Can I forget? NEVER! My experiences, and those of my fellow Holocaust survivors, can never be forgotten! Those hellish years will forever be a part of our bodies and souls. But we have made an effort to move on with our lives, some more successfully than others. We all suffered from post-traumatic stress disorder, but we didn't have a label for it at the time, and even if we did, there was no one waiting to help us. So we moved on. Despite the deplorable physical condition we were in, we were determined to be resilient and start our lives anew. We rebuilt our lives one small step at a time. I was, and still am, proud of my fellow survivors. We put all of our energy into rebuilding our lives. We survivors were weak physically, but not mentally. It took time, but we were able to bounce back with incredible vigor, displaying remarkable resilience.

Unbelievably, when World War II ended, many survivors, including myself, were forced to remain in displaced persons camps in the land of our worst enemy, Germany. People have often asked me about whether survivors wanted to take revenge and whether they ever did. After all that we had witnessed and experienced, it would have been a normal reaction to seek revenge, but when the war finally ended, we were first confronted with, and struck by, the enormity of our losses. We searched – usually in vain – for our family members and other survivors. Though we didn't know the number then, six million Jews had been murdered, including 1.5 million children. No revenge could ever diminish our pain or undo the wrong that had been done to us. Of course, there were some individual acts of revenge, but on the whole, survivors chose not to seek revenge. Instead they chose to move on with their lives, and that was my choice as well. It was a new beginning. Evil begets evil and we left it to governments to bring to justice those that committed the atrocities against us. However, as noted earlier, many of the perpetrators got away with minimal punishment, if any at all.

The lesson I wish for you, the reader, to learn is that there is a place in this world for everyone. When you witness an injustice, speak up. Open your hearts and minds to people of all religions, races, nationalities, sexual orientations, etc. Respect differences in people and learn from them. I have great hope that through books like this and many others, our loved ones will never be forgotten and that this generation, and future generations, will always strive to make this world a better place.

Zachor – Remember! Tikkun Olam – mend the world!

Editor's Note:

Sports writer Walter "Red" Smith once said, "There's nothing to writing. All you do is open a vein." And this can certainly be said about Ray's incredible accomplishment in writing Once We Were Eight.

I was blessed to be part of Ray's literary journey, and can attest to the fact that it was an extraordinary exercise for him. Adversity is one aspect of the human experience that most people want to forget – especially the type of adversity that Ray faced in his life. No one could possibly imagine how excruciating and ultimately how satisfying it has been for Ray to document his life story. What stands out for me are the many hours I spent with Ray going over and over every sentence, paragraph, and turn of phrase in his memoir. Ray made no effort to insulate himself from many painful memories. Every moment recalled dredged up more and more poignant and raw incidents to share. As if he was experiencing the opening of an old wound, Ray's eyes would well up with tears as he haltingly disclosed some new revelation. I would try to remain impassive, but the lump in my throat and a feeling of utter sadness would envelope me. Then, Ray would take a deep breath; quickly producing a handkerchief to dry his eyes. Each and every time he willed himself to go on and took me with him.

Ray started this book to keep his promise to his mother and provide a personal legacy to his children and grandchildren, but he has done much more than that. Ray's story stands as a testament to how one can not only survive unspeakable evil, loss and tragedy, but can thrive. Future generations of Fishlers will look back on Ray's life and take pride in the legacy he has left behind for them. As for me, I'm proud to call him my friend.

Mary Ann Cooper

Thank you for joining me on this literary journey.

If you wish to order another copy of *<u>Once We Were Eight</u>* for a family member or friend, please visit www.thebookpatch.com